Made Ready *in the* Fear Of The Lord

Preparing The Bride Of Christ For His Return

Tristan Stevenson-Coulshaw

Kingdom Publishers

Copyright© Tristan Stevenson-Coulshaw 2025

All rights reserved. No part of this book may be reproduced in any form by photocopying or any electronic or mechanical means, including information storage or retrieval systems, without permission in writing from both the copyright owner and the publisher of the book. The right of Tristan Stevenson-Coulshaw to be identified as the author of this work has been asserted by him in In accordance with the Copyright, Designs, and Patents Act 1988 and any subsequent amendments thereto.

A catalogue record for this book is available from the British Library.

All Scripture quotations have been taken from the New International and New living Translation Version of the Bible

ISBN: 978-1-916801-49-3

1st Edition 2025 by Kingdom Publishers, London, UK.

You can purchase copies of this book from any leading bookstore or at:

www.kingdompublishers.co.uk

Made Ready *in the* Fear of the Lord

Preparing the bride of Christ for His return

A theological and practical insight into understanding the fear of the Lord, its impact on everyday life and how it is key to preparing the Church for the return of Christ

Synopsis

The fear of the Lord is one of the most used phrases in the Bible, yet in recent decades there has been much confusion and disillusionment to what the fear of the Lord is and why we should fear Him. The Lord is restoring the fear of the Lord in these days and as we draw nearer to the return of Christ, the Church must and will grow in holiness, preparing herself for the Bridegroom's return.

Many people are crying out to the Lord for a revival and the fear of the Lord is a key value in this restoration of intimacy with God and in having a revived passion to reach the lost with an urgency and anxiety for their souls. May the fear of the Lord be revived in the hearts of God's holy people.

Contents

Foreword	9
Preface	12
Part 1: Introducing The Fear Of The Lord	**15**
Chapter 1 Preparing Your Hearts	17
Chapter 2 Intimate Friendship With God	20
Chapter 3 Knowing God's Heart To Protect His People	25
Part 2: Understanding The Fear Of The Lord	**28**
Chapter 4 The Importance Of The Fear Of The Lord	29
Chapter 5 The Revelation Of The Nature Of God Brings The Fear Of The Lord	38
Chapter 6 The Hatred Of Evil	43
Chapter 7 God's Righteous Anger	46
Chapter 8 What Does This Mean For The Believer?	49
Chapter 9 Key To Obedience	58
Part 3: The Fear Of The Lord In The Last Days	**62**
Chapter 10 A Dream	64
Chapter 11 A Prophetic Message	67
Chapter 12 The Return Of The King And His Coming Judgement	69
Chapter 13 What About The Believer's Judgement?	74
Chapter 14 What Will Happen In The Last Days?	80

Part 4: Practical Outworking   **84**

Chapter 15 A Daily Sign Of The Fear Of The Lord   **85**

Chapter 16 The Fear Of The Lord In Worship   **88**

Chapter 17 The Fear Of The Lord In Marriage   **93**

Chapter 18 The Fear Of The Lord In Family   **102**

Chapter 19 The Fear Of The Lord In The Workplace   **111**

Chapter 20 The Fear Of The Lord In Intercession   **114**

Chapter 21 The Fear Of The Lord In The Unifying Of Believers   **122**

Chapter 22 The Fear Of The Lord In Evangelism   **130**

Conclusion   **136**

Appendix 1: The Parables   **140**

Foreword

I believe this is a book which every Christian should read as the fear of the Lord is one of the first revelations a Christian disciple needs for them to remain obedient to the Lord and to His word.

I first met Tristan when he joined a Flame International mission to the Democratic Republic of Congo. He had just left the army and spent 40 days in the wilderness on Dartmoor seeking the Lord by reading and meditating on the word of God. I realised he was serious about his faith and hungry for the word of God, being able to recite long lengths of scripture the Lord had highlighted to him! He stood out as a radical Christian who loved Jesus and wanted only to be obedient. He attended All Nations Christian College and met his wife, Sarah. Since that time, he has worked within Flame in both a volunteer and employed capacity with the Next Generation, he has been a missionary in Greece with his family, he has led mission teams into Asia, he is an intercessor and has pioneered Flame Intercession Hubs for the nations. Tristan is a leader with a visionary prophetic ministry.

This book was birthed by revelation as Tristan prayed, read the scriptures and sought the Lord's face. He has a fear of the Lord which has equipped him with a passion to teach and impart it to the Body of Christ as he grasped the need for every Christian to walk with the Lord and to fear Him. This is a passion for both him and his family to walk out this revelation that he has been given to teach it at every opportunity. I watch him teaching his children bringing them up to fear the Lord and to understand just what an awesome Lord we serve.

Tristan is a man of God who walks out what he preaches. This means dying to self, putting God first, being obedient to the word of the Lord, keeping short accounts with Jesus and having clean hands and a pure heart. He is a risk taker for the Lord.

As a result of his passion, I have had revelation that we will see the Lord's glory in our land as we fear Him, as it says in Psalm 85:9, "Surely his salvation is near to those who fear him, so our land will be filled with his glory". I long to see our land filled with the glory of the Lord; I can only do that as I fear the Lord.

This is a journey that I believe we in Flame International are travelling along and we hope that as this important teaching is taken to the nations, we go with the healing ministry and this fear of the Lord. We believe it will be imparted to those to whom we minister, and salvation and healing will come and ultimately the Lord's glory will be revealed to the people and the land.

We are living in exciting times in the world, where there is a shift with increasing lawlessness and with greater activity of the Anti-Christ, and we, the believers in Jeshua, need to be ready for the return of the Messiah. I believe we are currently going through the "Birth Pangs of the last days", and it is a privilege to be alive.

We are at a time when we need to be alive to the Holy Spirit, be aware that we are carriers of the presence of God and as we approach the return of Jesus, we need to be ready. In 1 Thessalonians 5:23 Paul speaks of God's sanctification of our whole person. "May God himself, the God of peace, sanctify you through and through. May your whole spirit, soul and body be kept blameless at the coming of our Lord Jesus

Christ", talking about the end times. The time to be ready is NOW and if we do not have a fear of the Lord we could be caught napping, and this is not the way to receive the Messiah's return. We need to be keeping watch, challenging mindsets and breaking out of our comfort zones. The fear of the Lord will help us to keep watch. Pray for the Holy Spirit to impart this and seek the scriptures for those which refer to the fear of the Lord. Once you ask the Holy Spirit for the gift, I can tell you, the scriptures on this subject will continue to jump out at you and you will see the importance of the fear of the Lord!

It is my privilege to know Tristan and Sarah and their family well and I have seen their integrity, and I commend this book as I believe it is significant for the advancement of the Kingdom of God.

Lieutenant Colonel (Retired) Jan Ransom MBE
Founder, CEO and Director of Flame International

Preface

As an ex-serviceman in the British Army, I am well attuned to the command to "make ready!" With weapon in hand, the command to "make ready" prompts the soldier to immediately cock their weapon and attain the position of **watching out**: being ready for any approaching target. The rifle is fitted into the shoulder and their hands steadily hold the weapon. The soldier's eyes are fixed ahead as they wait for the target to reveal itself on the horizon. The soldier is not just aware of what might be coming….he is **ready**!

The bride of Christ, the Church, is to "make herself ready" for the Lord's return (Revelation 19:7). Is the Church ready for the return of Christ? Are you **made ready**? Are we attentive to the Day approaching, having fixed our eyes on Jesus and expectant of His soon return? Time is short and the Day of the Lord approaches quickly. How do we make ourselves ready, and how will we know we are ready? The Lord has given us a master key for being made ready for the return of Christ, and that is the fear of the Lord.

But what does it mean to fear the Lord, and is it really God's desire that we should fear Him?

In Hebrews 11:7 we are told, *"By faith Noah, when warned about things not yet seen, in holy fear built an ark to save his family."* We can learn much from our ancestor, Noah, in how the Church is to make herself ready for the coming judgement and return of Christ. Firstly, Noah was **warned** about the coming judgement and wrath of God on the earth, and in faith believed it to be true. If we fail to take heed of God's warning of His coming judgement when Christ returns, we cannot effectively prepare the Church, or in Noah's case, "build the ark". Noah's motive to build the ark, was **holy fear**. Noah knew that if He disobeyed God and did not prepare for the coming judgement, he and his family would also come under the wrath of that judgement. A holy fear gripped him to obey the Lord and escape God's wrath. But not only for himself, Noah built the ark to **save his family**. It is not just us who need to ensure we are prepared for the return of Christ, but our own family and our family in Christ, the growing Church across the nations.

This book is devoted to honour the Lord our God, *"Give unto the Lord the glory due to His name; worship the LORD in the beauty of holiness."* (Psalm 29:2 NKJV). It is also written to bless the Body of Christ, *"God has given each of you a gift from his great variety of spiritual gifts. Use them well to serve one another."* (1 Peter 4:10).

I write it in knowledge that one man can sow a seed, another can water it, but only God can make it grow. Perhaps you don't understand the concept of "fearing God", and in that case may this book sow seeds. Or perhaps you have known much about the fear of the Lord and do indeed have a holy fear of Him, in which case may this book water what has already been sown. But whether a man sows or waters is not important. What is important is that only God can make it grow. (1 Corinthians 3:7).

Therefore, I pray that God the Father will grant you the fear of the Lord. May He pour out upon you the Spirit of revelation and wisdom so that you may know Him better and be moved into His ways, which are holy. May your eyes be enlightened to see and witness the glory of the Lord that you may give Him the glory due His Name and worship Him acceptably in reverence and holy fear. May the Spirit of God move deeply upon you, transforming you more and more into the likeness and image of Christ. May Jesus, who holds us firmly in His grasp, lead you into intimate friendship with the Father and into the deeper riches of our glorious salvation and inheritance in Christ Jesus. To Him be the glory for ever and ever, Amen.

Part 1

Introducing The Fear Of The Lord

Let's be honest. When you hear the phrase "The fear of the Lord" – do you love it, or hate it? When someone says "Fear God" – what does that do inside you? Does it make your spirit leap in awe, and with an excited resound you say "Yes! Amen!", or is there a sense of turning in your stomach and wrestling in your mind, causing something within you to cringe at the statement and concept of it? Or perhaps neither, and there is an emptiness of emotion, yet an intrigue to peer through the lens of scripture and seek why we should have a holy fear of God.

The term, 'the fear of the Lord' has unfortunately received much of a bad name in western Christendom in recent decades. Many seem to have permanently replaced the word "fear" with "awe", quickly saying, "The fear of the Lord does not actually mean to fear Him, but to be in awe of Him", and would rather have the word "fear" removed from scripture. This may be partly due to some abuse of the term, but I expect it is more about a lack of knowledge of God and therefore, not understanding why we should have a holy fear of Him.

The awe of the Lord is indeed an element of the fear of the Lord, but it is important for us to have a holy fear of God; a fear that does not cause us to run away from Him, but causes us to ***run towards Him***, in holy fear!

Whatever your current standpoint, can I ask you to suspend some thoughts and seek a fresh revelation of this topic. Here, we ultimately address theology (our perception and understanding of God), and though this is not my purpose, it inevitably will do. The more important outcome I hope for you will be to deepen your reverential attitude towards God and that through this transformation we will live more holy, pleasing and fruitful lives for His Kingdom and glory. May the bride make herself ready for His coming!

Chapter 1
Preparing Your Hearts

Perhaps a reason for why some believers wrestle with the concept of fearing God, is because they believe it is in opposition with the love and grace of God. This is not the case. It is imperative for the believer to receive the incredible love and grace of God and to pursue knowing this for themselves. If we have been brought up, perhaps with very disciplinarian parents, we may be inclined to read this topic through the eyes of "I'm only loved and accepted by my father or mother if I do good things". This, of course, can cause the believer to lean towards the belief of salvation based on works, rather than by grace. Believers with this tendency may often be captive to 'perfectionism', thus reading this book through those eyes could make them feel like a constant failure in the eyes of God, and never enough.

It is important to recognise there is also a godly desire for 'Christian perfection', but one can distinguish this from ungodly perfectionism through the presence of **faithful love**. What I mean is this: One person can pursue Christian perfection, driven with a holy fear but always knowing that Father God is **FOR** them, cheering them on, forgiving their faults, disciplining in love, and *encouraging* them to mature. Another person though, can pursue Christian perfection, driven with a fear believing that Father God is **AGAINST** them, waiting for them to make a mistake and then severely punishing them and 'tutting' them when they do. It is important for us, therefore, to be jointly rooted in the grace and love of God as we walk in the fear of God.

Let us take a moment then to remember that God wants to help you run the Christian race well, and even when we slip up or run off course, He wants to bring you back on course that you may continue to run the race well.

If you are a believer and follower of Jesus Christ, you are so because God the Father wanted you to be. It has very little to do with you at all; you are saved because **He wanted you saved!** Jesus says in John 6:44, *"No one can come to me unless the Father who sent me draws them"*. It is common for people to find it more difficult to receive Father God's love than Jesus Christ's love, and that is often due to painful experiences from our earthly parents. But what Jesus says in the above verse is amazing. **It wasn't Jesus's decision to save you; it was the Father's.**

No one can come to Jesus unless the Father draws them to Him. Our salvation originates from the Father. It was Father God who wanted to redeem mankind to Himself. It was Father God who wanted a family of people. It was Father God who sent Jesus, His Son, to do it! And it is Jesus who leads us back to the Father. Our salvation originates from the Father, and the purpose of our salvation is for the Father. *"For there is one God, the Father, by whom all things were made, and for whom we live."* (1 Corinthians 8:6). Jesus said that He Himself is the *way*, and He is the way to the destination. He Himself is not the destination, but the way *to* the destination. The destination is the Father! Jesus said, *"I am the way, the truth and the life. No one comes to the Father, except through me."* (John 14:6).

Let that sink in. God, the Father, loves you and has called you to know His Son so that you may be saved and brought up into God's family.

So much is the love of God for you, that He now calls you His child. Now you are His child, He will treat you like His child, and He will be like a Father to you.

Some might then question; "How does love and fear work together? Surely if God loves me, I don't need to fear Him." But now we have received the grace of God and are adopted into His family, we are called to walk in sanctification, becoming more like Christ. This, as you will see throughout this book, is largely done through the fear of the Lord. Proverbs 16:6 says, "Through love and faithfulness *sin is atoned for*; through the fear of the LORD *evil is avoided.*"

Chapter 2
Intimate Friendship With God

Let me begin also by encouraging you. There are many blessings revealed in scripture for those who fear the Lord, and we will address many throughout this book, but one that I want to hold on to from the beginning is the blessing of growing in deep and intimate friendship with the Lord.

Psalm 25:14 says, *"The friendship of the LORD is for those who fear him, and he makes known to them his covenant."* (ESV)

Other translations say, "The LORD confides in those who fear him" (NIV), and "The secret of the LORD *is* with those who fear him" (NKJV).

The fear of the Lord blesses us with a deep friendship with God to the extent that He chooses to confide in those who fear Him and intimately reveal His secrets and ways to them.

God wants us to know Him! He shares this truth in many ways, but through the prophet Hosea He says, *"I want you to show love, not offer sacrifices. **I want you to know me** more than I want burnt offerings."* (Hosea 6:6). Likewise, in John 17:3 we see that eternal life is "to know the only true God, and Jesus Christ". This is a wonderful invitation of the Lord. In this, His desire for relationship and friendship are evident. But the Lord confides in **those who fear him**. If we don't have a holy and true fear of Him, we will not have the fullness of friendship with Him that He offers us, and instead we can go through our Christian lives not living with the intimacy and blessing that is at hand for us because our relationship with Him has not included the fear of the Lord.

Have you considered that a reason why you may be missing out on blessings and friendship with God is because you don't have a holy fear of Him? Many Christians can pass through their lives knowing God's love for them, being thankful for their salvation, doing wonderful deeds for the Lord and enjoy times of experiencing His goodness, yet still miss out on something much deeper and more intimate. God is inviting us into a deeper knowledge of who He is and if received and taken to heart, this promises to open up a friendship with Him and an awareness of His glory that you may not have yet experienced or didn't believe were possible.

What we have to bear in mind as we grow in our knowledge of God, is that God is not the one who changes – we are! Jesus is the same yesterday, today and forever (Hebrews 13:8). Our theology of Him is not perfect; He is perfect! As we pursue a relationship with Him, seeking greater revelation and wisdom, we have to be willing to submit our theology and feelings about God to the revelation of scripture. All scripture has been God-breathed and the Holy Spirit speaks through God's word. If we don't like or disagree with something in God's word, we must be careful not to reshape it to fit our understanding of God but rather transform our minds to become more and more into the image and likeness of Christ.

As we begin to talk on this subject of the fear of the Lord, let us first address a simple reality of recognising two different aspects of God: His "soft" side, and His "hard" side. Have grace for my earthly use of words, but for the purpose of explaining the different aspects of Him, I will use the phrases "soft" and "hard".

The soft elements of God's nature and character are perhaps more palatable to the human soul; His love, mercy, goodness, kindness, gentleness and grace. The harder aspects of God's character and ways are probably less palatable; His anger, vengeance, hatred, judgement and holiness. Now, if we only consider one aspect of what God is like, for example, His goodness and grace, then we will have a narrow and incomplete revelation of who He is. In fact, I would go as far to say that if we believed God only encompassed one of those sides and not both, either the "soft" side, or the "hard" side, then we would have a deceived perception of who He is.

We are encouraged by the Spirit to *"consider the kindness **and severity** of God"* (Romans 11:22). Therefore, if we really want to know God better and fall in love with the fullness of who He is, we need to seek both sides of what He is like. On one hand He builds, and on the other He destroys. On one hand He loves, and on the other hand, He hates. On one hand He has forgiving mercy, and on the other He unleashes fiery judgement. On one hand He creates peace and on the other hand He makes war. On one hand He brings unity, and on the other hand He brings a sword of division. It's what He is like, and He doesn't change.

It's too easy for the human mind to think of characteristics of God that we don't recognise in Him and say, "That's not the Jesus I know, therefore it's not the real Jesus." It is quite the opposite; if you are confronted with some characteristic or ways of God in scripture which you do not yet relate to, the response is not that Jesus is wrong but that you need to know the Jesus of the Bible better.

As we read scriptures and seek insight into them throughout this book, we should remember that He is the same, yesterday, today and forever.

He does not change! It is we who change and even our view and understanding of Him must be willing to change in accordance with the word of God so that we can relate with the unchanging God and Creator better!

In order for our friendship with the Lord to go deeper, we need to relate with Him knowing both His soft and hard sides. In fact, I believe ***it is in relating with the harder aspects of God that we get drawn into deeper friendship with Him.***

Let's consider that statement on a human level. With some friends we relate on a shallow level, and with other friends our friendship goes very deep. We have both shallow and deep friendships. What defines the difference between these relationships? Friendship is a physical, emotional and spiritual bond and either it is shallow, or it goes deep. Now I'm not talking about sharing your vulnerabilities with professionals, like doctors, but consider those with whom you are friends.

When I asked a friend and colleague of mine for what the difference is between a shallow and deep friendship, I think her answer nailed it on the head. "My deep friends are those I can really trust. Those who I can even trust with the deep things going on in my heart. When I am hurting and feeling angry or frustrated on the inside, I can share it with them as I know they will be able to listen to me and understand. I wouldn't share these things with those I have shallow friendships with, as I wouldn't trust their motives or reactions".

This, I believe is how God sees us too! Moses had such a wonderful friendship with the Lord that it has been noted that God spoke with him face to face, as one speaks to a friend (Exodus 33:11). But what did God talk to Moses about? God often confided in Moses, sharing with him how He felt and what God wanted to do about it. This is enormously intimate of God; to share with mere man about His emotions! Often these emotions were anger, disappointment or regret (Exodus 32:7-14, Numbers 14:11-20). I can't help but be in awe at the vulnerability of our God, sharing such things. But God trusted Moses with this intimacy of friendship because He knew Moses feared God and revered Him.

I would like you to hold this hope in your heart and mind as you read through this book; that there can be much greater depth of intimacy with God for those who fear Him.

Chapter 3
Knowing God's Heart To Protect His People

Another aspect I want to share before we get into the meat of this book, is something the Lord shared with me in a time I was wrestling with whether it was right for me to preach on the fear of the Lord. I wanted to know the Lord's purpose behind giving me this message.

There was a time in 2022 when I was teaching on the fear of the Lord on an online course for Flame International and also in a House Church in Lesvos, Greece, to largely young missionaries. It was an intense season of teaching, even more as I was teaching on this 'heavy & intense', 'controversial' and perhaps 'uncomfortable' topic. I was very aware that much of this teaching could appear to grind against the preaching of "only grace" which is common in the Western evangelical church, and at some point in this heavy season of preaching on the fear of the Lord I was brought to my knees, desperately seeking the Lord's counsel as to why I was preaching this tough message and if it was indeed "right" to preach it.

"Lord, is this truly right for me to talk on this topic to your people? Many are young believers, and many are older and wiser than I am. Is this really what you want me to share with them? Lord Jesus, I need to know your heart, for what you want to be doing with your people through this message. What's your desire Lord; what's your intention for your people through this message? Because if I am not doing this from your heart and purpose for them, then I don't want to be doing it."

The response came immediately, "I want to protect them." I knew I was being directed to Jesus's prayer recorded in John 17 and as I was turning through the pages I knew from the Holy Spirit that I was to read Jesus's prayer, taking note of the specific requests in His prayer, as most of the words Jesus is conversing with His Father are about other things and not actually requesting or asking for anything. I was amazed at what I saw.

In Jesus's prayer for His disciples and for all believers (John 17:6-26), Jesus has seven requests. It is important to recognise these specific requests because when we see the request as the gathered conclusion of what He is speaking with His Father about, we can understand His heart's desires, through His prayer. Jesus spends the first five verses (v.6-10) conversing with the Father, but in verse 11 it results in His first and foundational request for His disciples. *"Holy Father, **protect them**, by the power of your name, the name you gave me, so that they will be one, as you and I are one."* Jesus next goes on to give His second request to the Father in verse 15. *"I'm not asking you to take them out of the world, but to **protect them from the evil one**."* Two verses later in verse 17, Jesus then gives His third and fourth request to the Father *"**Make them holy...teach them your word**."*

It is valuable to see what Jesus is really crying out to the Father for, regarding His precious flock. As Jesus is crying out to God for them, His foundational and primary prayer is to **protect them!** Jesus is the Good Shepherd of His flock. In His incomparable love for us, just as a Father wants to guard his family, so Jesus wants to protect His flock.

But protect them from what? **Protect them from the evil one** (v15). What does this mean? It means to **make them holy** (v17), because to be holy means to be set apart, to have nothing to do with sin or evil, to not give in to temptation of sin or be lured into deception, but to remain wholeheartedly committed to God and His holy ways.

Though perhaps not entirely relevant, (but incredibly insightful), as we carry on reading Jesus's famous prayer in the latter half of John 17 (v20-26), Jesus's three requests are all for unity. One example is, *"I pray that they will be one, just as you and I are one – as you are in me, Father, and I am in you...." (v21)*. But the Lord revealed to me something wonderful about unity that day that I had never seen or known before. In verse 11, Jesus prays, *"Holy Father, **protect them**, by the power of your name, the name you gave me, **so that they will be one**, as you and I are one."* The "way" or "means" to unity in the Body of Christ is to be protected from the evil one and sin (to be holy!). This makes perfect sense! The Body of Christ will be one, as Christ is in the Father and the Father is in Christ, when we are protected from evil and set-apart from the ways of the world. **Holiness brings unity!**

When we are acting in sin, we are uniting ourselves with evil, and when we do that we forsake our unity with Christ. For there is no unity between Christ and the devil (2 Corinthians 6:15).

Know therefore, that as we focus in this book on the fear of the Lord, something of the Lord's intention is to protect Christ's special flock from the evil one, and the fear of the Lord is absolutely key in protecting us from evil! For *"by fearing the Lord, people avoid evil."* (Proverbs 16:6).

Part 2

Understanding The Fear Of The Lord

Chapter 4
The Importance Of The Fear Of The Lord

The true importance of something can only be assessed by the measure to which God values it Himself.

This is, I believe, is a foundational question; is the fear of the Lord important to God? If so, how important? Then we should consider our response; if it matters to God, it must matter to us. Every believer has choices to do things, seek things, desire things that either draws us nearer to God, or further from Him. And as we grow more and more into Christ, we find that what is important to Him becomes more important to us, and what is not important to Him becomes less important to us.

Let us consider then, how important it is to God, for us to have a holy fear of Him. Let's look at seven aspects.

1: God requires us to fear Him

As God is revealing Himself and His ways to the people of Israel, Moses speaks to them and informs them about what God requires, "And now, Israel, what does the Lord your God require of you? He requires only that you *fear the Lord your God*, and live in a way that pleases him, and love him and serve him with all your heart and soul" – Deuteronomy 10:12. At the heart of these instructions God is plainly expressing to His people that He is their God. We are in a God-people relationship, not a God-God or a people-people relationship, and so He is explaining some of the foundational facts about what being in relationship with God is all about. There are four aspects here that God requires of His people:

1. Fear Him
2. Live in a way that pleases Him
3. Love Him
4. Serve Him with all your heart and soul

These are not unnecessary rules that God chooses to give us; they are an insight into His heart for what is important to Him in our relationship with Him. God wants the most intimate, full relationship with us, and He graciously gives us the "keys" to this close relationship. We may consider it easy to grasp points 2,3 & 4; to live in a way that pleases Him, to love Him and serve Him but let us not forget the first and foundational requirement – to fear Him! *He requires **ONLY** that you fear the Lord your God, **AND** ….the others.* Let's not think that our relationship with God has changed so much since our redemption in Christ that we should rule out one of the basic principles of our relationship with God. If we rule out one, why not rule out the others and consider that because we are saved in Christ we no longer need to live in a way that pleases God, or love Him or serve Him, because it's all been done for us in Jesus! Be careful flock, of such deception. *"Dear children, do not let anyone lead you astray. The one who does what is right is righteous, just as he is righteous."* (1 John 3:7)

What this is beginning to reveal to us is that the fear of the Lord is a foundational component of our right relationship with Him. We can't truly do the other bits (live pleasing lives, love and serve Him) without having that foundation layer, which is the fear of the Lord.

The primary importance of fearing God is seen in many other places in the Scriptures, but let's look at one more. 1 Samuel 12:14 says, *"Now if you fear and worship the Lord and listen to his voice, and if you do not rebel against the Lord's commands, then both you and your king will show that you recognise the Lord as your God."*

Again, we are given a list of right-living and approach to God. The primary importance is to fear Him, worship Him, and listen and obey. It's very simple really – adopt these four spiritual ways, and you will identify yourself with God. The issue is often when people seek to worship, listen, and obey without it being grounded on the foundation of fearing Him!

2: God wants the whole world to fear Him

Psalm 33 is a beautiful Psalm which between verses 6-9 (below) highly exalts God the Creator:

> *By the word of the Lord the heavens were made,*
> *their starry host by the breath of his mouth.*
> *He gathers the waters of the sea into jars;*
> *he puts the deep into storehouses.*
> *Let all the earth fear the Lord;*
> *let all the people of the world revere him.*
> *For he spoke, and it came to be;*
> *he commanded, and it stood firm.*

As we are invited into a God-perspective of how the heavens and earth were made we see the natural response the earth has. *"Let all the earth fear the Lord; let all the people of the world revere him"*. Why? *"For he spoke, and it came to be; he commanded, and it stood firm"*. This is the world's response to the Creator – to fear and have a deep reverence of Him. When we come into the revelation of the power and magnitude of God Our Creator, our response will be a fear and reverence of Him. The Psalmist goes on to proclaim the following words in vs 10-11:

> *The Lord foils the plans of the nations;*
> *he thwarts the purposes of the peoples.*
> *But the plans of the Lord stand firm forever,*
> *the purposes of his heart through all generations.*

In these verses we are in awe of the God who does what He wants to; foiling the plans of nations and thwarting the purposes of the peoples. There is no point trying to work against Him. In fact, our awe of Him should drive us to want to work with Him, for His plans and purposes shall prosper.

3: God's purpose is for us to fear Him

Again, as we seek to know the heart of God we are invited into the plans and purposes of His heart. God's purpose is what really matters and when we know His purposes, we can understand Him more. God has several purposes that are revealed to us in scripture, but one of them is indeed for the whole world to fear Him. Ecclesiastes 3:14 is in the context of King Solomon recognising that God, above all things, is God. He will do as He pleases; *"And I know that whatever God does is final. Nothing can be added to it or taken from it.* ***God's purpose is that people should fear Him****"*.

It is a humbling thought to also ask what purposes God has for doing things in our lives. What are His purposes for blessing us? What are His purposes for bringing us through trials and hardships? There may be several purposes, or motives, to God blessing us, but one is certainly so that the whole world will fear Him! As is seen in Psalm 67:6-7, *"The land yields its harvest; God, our God, blesses us.* ***May God bless us still, SO THAT all the ends of the earth will fear him"***. God wants the world to fear Him!

4: The fear of the Lord is the beginning and the conclusion

This revelation of King Solomon continues in the book of Ecclesiastes. King Solomon had been gifted by God with wisdom and understanding "beyond measure". One of the revelations of wisdom that was given to him is that "The fear of the LORD is the beginning of wisdom" – Proverbs 9:10a. The NLT translation puts it that the "fear of the Lord is the foundation of wisdom". If we don't have the fear of the Lord then what "wisdom" do we actually have? All wisdom is founded on and begins with the fear of the Lord. Then, as King Solomon expresses the truth and challenges of having such wisdom in the book of Ecclesiastes, he comes not just to "a" conclusion, but "the" conclusion of humanity.

Ecclesiastes 12:8-15 says,

"Everything is meaningless," says the Teacher, "completely meaningless."

Keep this in mind: The Teacher was considered wise, and he taught the people everything he knew. He listened carefully to many proverbs, studying and classifying them. The Teacher sought to find just the right words to express truths clearly. The words of the wise are like cattle prods—painful but helpful. Their collected sayings are like a nail-studded stick with which a shepherd drives the sheep.

But, my child, let me give you some further advice: Be careful, for writing books is endless, and much study wears you out.

That's the whole story. Here now is my final conclusion: Fear God and obey his commands, for this is everyone's duty. *God will judge us for everything we do, including every secret thing, whether good or bad.*

Not only does wisdom reveal to us that the fear of the Lord is both the beginning AND the conclusion of all wise living but teaches us that it is our duty. What's more, is that King Solomon reveals the ultimate reason for why we fear God. It all boils down to, *"God will judge us for everything we do, including every secret thing, whether good or bad."*

5: God delights in the fear of the Lord

We are speaking on the matter of finding what is important in God's eyes. Another way we can phrase 'what is important', is 'what He delights in'. In the same way that some things are more important to God than other things, we can know that some things cause more delight to God than other things, and we should consider that whatever God delights in is important to Him! It is wonderful to know that we are loved by Him but the revelation of knowing what God delights in causes us to eagerly seek it so that we can be on the other end of what God delights in. Psalm 147:11 expresses *"The Lord's delight is in those who fear him, those who put their hope in his unfailing love."*. Other translations say "The Lord takes pleasure" or "The Lord is pleased with" or "The Lord favours" those who fear him. (ESV, BSB, NASB)

As I mentioned in the introduction, the fear of the Lord in no way takes away the love of God. In fact, they work perfectly together and this scripture is so wonderful as it comes to terms with the two attributes that God desires for His people: To fear Him and have hope in His unfailing love. They can work together, and they do work together. In Psalm 33:18 we have a similar revelation *"The Lord watches over those who fear him, those who rely on his unfailing love"*. It is undeniable that God has a special delight for those who fear Him. It is set-apart as something divinely special and important.

6: The fear of the Lord is "key" to His treasure

Isaiah prophesied, "The Lord is exalted, for he dwells on high; he will fill Zion with his justice and righteousness. He will be the sure foundation for your times, a rich store of salvation and wisdom and knowledge; the fear of the Lord is the key to this treasure." (Isaiah 33:5-6)

Isaiah mentions that the Lord is our foundation. This is further recited in 1 Corinthians 3:11, declaring that Jesus Christ is our foundation. Isaiah then goes on to say that the Lord is "a **rich store** of salvation and wisdom and knowledge". These are the great treasures God has for His people. And what is the key to this treasure? The fear of the Lord!

7: The fear of the Lord is the delight of Jesus

What astounds me is to see the relationship between Jesus and the Father. Jesus and the Father are One, and they are One in Spirit. Isaiah prophecies much about the great revelation of the coming Messiah. One revelation that God gave Isaiah was the fullness of the Spirit of God resting on the Messiah. The fullness of the Holy Spirit is phrased as the "Sevenfold Spirit" or the "Seven Spirits of God" *(Revelation 1:4 & 5:6)* and where this phrase stems from is the revelation of the "Seven Spirits of God" that Isaiah prophesied in Isaiah 11:1-3.

Here we read of the fullness of the Holy Spirit (the Seven Spirits) marking Jesus as the anointed one of God, the Messiah.

> *A shoot will come up from the stump of Jesse;*
> *from his roots a Branch will bear fruit.*
> *The Spirit of the Lord (1) will rest on him —*
> *the Spirit of wisdom (2) and of understanding (3),*
> *the Spirit of counsel (4) and of might (5),*
> *the Spirit of the knowledge (6) and fear of the Lord (7) —*
> *and he will delight in the fear of the Lord.*
>
> (Isaiah 11:1-3a)

As Isaiah is given this prophetic revelation from God on the fullness and wholeness of God's Spirit that will rest on the Messiah, God makes special notice, a special declaration from the secrets of Heaven that it is this one component, this final element that deserves extra special attention – that of all the seven Spirits of God resting on Jesus, it is the last one that causes greatest pleasure: "**and he will delight in the fear of the Lord**".

In Hebrew understanding, seven represents fullness, wholeness and completion. When this occurs in Scripture, we also learn that the seventh of the seven things is often regarded as particularly important. Consider the seven days of the week, and the seventh (the day God rested), is set-apart as holy. In a different view, we are informed of seven things that God particularly hates (Proverbs 6:16-19). The scripture says, "Six things the Lord hates, seven which are an abomination to him". This means that the first six, the Lord hates, but the seventh has a great emphasis on it; "it is an abomination".

This is the same with Isaiah's scripture; that the seventh of the Seven Spirits, the Spirit of the fear of the Lord, has extra honour, it is His delight.

With all this in mind we cannot escape the reality of how important the fear of the Lord is to God. This alone is enough reason for us to choose to fear God; because He demands it of us and He loves it! We should journey forward with great expectancy and also a deep reverence as we seek more insight into the fear of the Lord and how to obtain it.

If at any point whilst reading this book you lose motivation to complete it or lose inspiration to seek the fear of the Lord, you may be encouraged by ***returning to this chapter!***

The true importance of something can only be assessed by the measure to which God values it Himself.

Chapter 5
The Revelation Of The Nature Of God Brings The Fear Of The Lord

Let's start with a question: What do you think your reaction would be if God turned up in your living room? What do you think you would do? Your answer will reveal something about your personal belief and current revelation of God's nature.

The best place in the entire universe, I believe, to seek the revelation of the nature of God is in the midst of His presence, in the Most Holy Place, where God sits on the throne. Both Isaiah and the Apostle John were taken up to the Most Holy Place in Heaven to witness the vision of the awesome presence of God. This is John's revelation taken from Revelation 4:2-8.

"At once I was in the Spirit, and there before me was a throne in heaven with someone sitting on it. And the one who sat there had the appearance of jasper and ruby. A rainbow that shone like an emerald encircled the throne. Surrounding the throne were twenty-four other thrones, and seated on them were twenty-four elders. They were dressed in white and had crowns of gold on their heads. From the throne came flashes of lightning, rumblings and peals of thunder. In front of the throne, seven lamps were blazing. These are the

seven spirits of God. Also in front of the throne there was what looked like a sea of glass, clear as crystal.

In the centre, around the throne, were four living creatures, and they were covered with eyes, in front and in back. The first living creature was like a lion, the second was like an ox, the third had a face like a man, the fourth was like a flying eagle. Each of the four living creatures had six wings and was covered with eyes all around, even under its wings. Day and night they never stop saying:

> **"Holy, holy, holy**
> **is the Lord God Almighty,**
> **who was, and is, and is to come."**

Isaiah spoke a little more about these four living creatures who surround the throne and identifies them as mighty seraphim. God has positioned them over His Throne and there they remain, day and night. As they fly over the Throne, in the almighty presence of God and His glory, they use two of their wings to cover their eyes, two of their wings to cover their feet, and the last two to fly with. They are so impacted by His glory that they have to cover their eyes and feet with their wings and cry out to one another the only thing that they can really cry out when standing in the unveiled presence of God;

> **"Holy, holy, holy is the LORD Almighty".**

The highest revelation of the nature of God is that He is holy. The living creatures surrounding His throne are not moved by His glorious presence to cry out day and night, "Loving, loving, loving is the Lord God Almighty", or "Good, good, good is the Lord God Almighty". They cry out "Holy, holy, holy" because that is who He is!

Let's not deny God's love or His goodness. GOD IS LOVE, and God is good! But above all things, His nature and presence reveal holiness. I do not personally believe that God has commanded the mighty seraphim to say these words. I do not believe God has given them a script to cry out over Him day and night. I do not believe it is a command that they say these things; **I believe it is a revelation!**

If we were to see the unveiled almighty presence of God, I believe we would, by the impact of His manifest glory, do the same thing. Let us think of Jesus, the image of the invisible God, who is the full manifestation of God's glory. When we think of Jesus, how do you picture Him? Do we picture something along the lines of what He probably looked like while He was on the earth doing His ministry? Brown hair, thick beard, white shepherd's gown with a brown belt round His waist? But why would we focus our attention on the pre-glorified and victorious Lord? Let's gaze upon His beauty as He is now – the once crucified and now risen Lord, who has ascended into heaven and has sat down in the seat of honour at the right hand of the Father. That's who we're united with; the risen and glorified Jesus who reigns in Heaven.

The once crucified, risen and ascended Lord reveals Himself to the Apostle John, recorded in Revelation 1. Let us look at His image in vs12-16.

"I turned around to see the voice that was speaking to me. And when I turned I saw seven golden lampstands, and among the lampstands was someone like a son of man, dressed in a robe reaching down to his feet and with a golden sash around his chest. The hair on his head was white like wool, as white as snow, and his eyes were like blazing fire. His feet were like bronze glowing in a furnace, and his voice was like the sound of rushing waters. In his right hand he held seven stars, and coming out of his mouth was a sharp, double-edged sword. His face was like the sun shining in all its brilliance."

Before this, the Apostle John had known and loved Jesus, enjoying the benefits of a close relationship with Him, even known as the one who had laid his head on the bosom of Christ and the one who was known as "the one whom Jesus loved" (John 20:2). It is undeniable that the Apostle John had an incredibly deep and intimate friendship with Jesus, yet when John saw Jesus appearing now, in more of His manifest glory, he "fell at his feet as though dead" (v.17). This was the reaction the disciple whom Jesus loved had, when Jesus stepped into his living room because for the first time, He had a greater revelation of the fullness of Christ and who He is. John undoubtedly knew Jesus as His friend, His Shepherd, His Master and His Saviour, but here, Jesus is revealing Himself as the Judge and He who inflicts the vengeance and wrath of God on the earth.

The revelation of Christ as Judge gives us a holy fear of Him

Jesus Christ is the judge. *"Moreover, the Father judges no one, but has entrusted all judgment to the Son, that all may honour the Son just as they honour the Father."* (1 John 5:22-23)

This same image of Jesus in Revelation 1 was revealed to the prophet Daniel in His vision of the Ancient of Days, recorded in Daniel 7:9 *"As I looked, thrones were set in place and the Ancient of Days took his seat. His clothing was as white as snow; the hair of his head was white like wool. His throne was flaming with fire, and its wheels were all ablaze."* The context of this image is judgement, (vs 10) *"The court was seated, and the books were opened."*

Another confirmation that this image of Christ reveals Himself as the Judge is that *"out of his mouth was a double-edged sword."* This is revealed further in Revelation 19:15; *"From his mouth comes a sharp sword with which to strike down the nations, and he will rule them with a rod of iron. He will tread the winepress of the fury of the wrath of God the Almighty."*

This of course is a picture of the fulfilment of the prophecy of Christ written in Psalm 2:9 *"You will break them with a rod of iron; you will dash them to pieces like pottery."*

In holy fear this Psalm should compel churches to pray that the kings and rulers of our nations have the fear of God for we know something of the terror of the Lord that they don't!

We will look at this theme of judgement later on, but it's important that we consider "What is our view of King Jesus?" Is it of a humble and gentle King, entering Jerusalem on a colt, or is it of a Warrior King, riding into Jerusalem on a warhorse? He is both! Too many people only know the humble and gentle side of Jesus as Saviour, and do not know much of Jesus as Lord and Judge.

We should desire to know the fullness of who Jesus is; He is Saviour, and Judge, but too many don't know His judgement or have a holy fear of Him. I believe now is the time the Lord is strongly calling His Church to return to the fear of the Lord.

Chapter 6
The Hatred Of Evil

A very basic, but absolute key to understanding the fear of the Lord is revealed in Proverbs 8:13. *"The fear of the Lord is hatred of evil."*

This goes hand in hand with the highest revelation of the nature of God, spoken of in the previous chapter; that God is holy. God is totally set apart from wickedness and evil, *"God is light, and in him there is no darkness at all."* (1 John 1:5)

I don't think it will take much convincing for the believer to agree with me that God is holy and in Him there is no evil at all, but perhaps it doesn't sit as comfortably to consider that God is full of hatred towards evil!

It is easy for us to meditate on God's love, but have you meditated much on God's hatred? In your growing relationship with God, you may joyfully open your heart to be filled with His love, but how much do you open your heart to be filled with His hatred?

One might say, "Isn't that a contradiction in terms?" "Isn't hatred itself evil, so therefore there is no hatred in the heart of God, for the scriptures declare, "God is love"?" But if God truly is love, and if God truly is good, He must therefore, hate evil. For if God *loves* justice, He must therefore *hate* injustice, and if God *loves* truth, He must therefore *hate* lies.

I believe that in God's fair and just nature, the proportion to which God loves, He also hates. The case is not, "God loves justice, but only dislikes injustice a little bit." That isn't logical, loving or just. In a similar way, I could not think of my wife and say that I love her faithfulness towards me in marriage and am jealous for her love, to then be ok with the thought of her walking off with another man! That's absurd! I can't love the marital faithfulness of my wife and not equally hate the thought of any marital unfaithfulness!

A concern I have for the Body of Christ right now is that we do not "hate" very well. Our pursuit of love and grace has caused many to approve and accept what God hates. Tolerating evil is not a part of God's ways. We should have grace and love for the sinner but hate the sin. Sometimes it can be hard to differentiate the two. You can spend time with the person, and have grace and love for them, but that does not mean that you quench the fire of the Holy Spirit that burns within you. Do we burn with a holy desire for sinners to be deeply convicted of their sin and "cut to the heart"? Do we cry out to God for mercy because you know His hatred of evil, or do you speak with God about them like their sin is no big deal?

Where there are issues of sin which are being widely accepted in the church today, you have to make a choice. Do you fully embrace the sin, or totally reject it? It is not good to be on the fence about such things, saying "I don't fully approve, nor do I fully reject". That is lukewarmness, and the Word of God warns us that the lukewarm will be spat out the mouth of Christ (Revelation 3:16). Holiness does not mean to be on the fence so that you can be friends with the world and friends with God, for *"Friendship with the world is enmity towards God"* (James 4:4). I grieve and tremble for the lack of the fear of the Lord in the Church today! If we do not hate what God hates, then either we do not know God, or we have chosen to be lukewarm, or even against Him. I believe the Lord continues to challenge us not to be embarrassed that the God whom we love and serve, hates evil and sin, and like Him, we also need to *"hate all that is evil."* (Romans 12:9).

Chapter 7
God's Righteous Anger

When we experience more revelation of God's hatred of evil, we simultaneously draw nearer to His emotion of "righteous anger". You cannot comprehend God's hatred of evil without your heart being impacted with God's emotion of righteous and holy anger that burns against such evil, for *"Our God is a consuming fire"* (Hebrews 12:29).

Let us remember Jesus releasing His anger at the market traders in the temple. In John 2:13-17.

"When the Jewish Passover was near, Jesus went up to Jerusalem. In the temple courts He found men selling cattle, sheep, and doves, and money changers seated at their tables. So He made a whip out of cords and drove all from the temple courts, both sheep and cattle. He poured out the coins of the money changers and overturned their tables. To those selling doves He said, 'Get these out of here! How dare you turn My Father's house into a marketplace'. His disciples remembered that it is written: "Zeal for Your house will consume Me.'!"" (John 2:13-17 BSB)

The scripture that the disciples remembered *"Zeal for Your house will consume me"* is written in Psalm 69:9, and this is what they saw in Christ at this moment of anger. The Greek word for zeal - *'zelos'* - means to burn with emotion, or to have an 'inner feeling boiling over'.

The root word *'ze'* literally means "hot enough to boil" and is metaphorically used of "burning anger, love, zeal".

Thus, a burning love for God's house matched with a hatred of lawlessness and sin, brought Jesus to burn with anger as He turned the tables and used His whip to drive the animals out of the temple.

So not only do we have a God who hates evil, but His hatred of evil and sin can cause Him to burn with anger, and in the right time, He then acts in judgement or wrath. This is why He is to be feared. Psalm 90:11 says, "Who can comprehend the power of your anger? Your wrath is as awesome as the fear you deserve."

It is good that God is slow to anger and is patient, because otherwise there would be no world right now!

God's fiery judgement

Much of the fear of the Lord comes from a holy and cautious fear of God's judgement. When we have a holy fear of God's judgement, we have the fear of the Lord. The clearest understanding of this I believe, is in Jesus's words Himself. Luke 12:4-5, *"Dear friends, don't be afraid of those who want to kill your body; they cannot do any more to you after that. But I'll tell you whom to fear. Fear God, who has the power to kill you and then throw you into hell. Yes, he's the one to fear."*

Jesus is putting things as bluntly as can be! He is not talking to unbelievers, He is talking to His twelve disciples, His friends. He tells them why **they** are to fear God, and that is because He has the power to kill them and throw them into hell. The fear of God can mean several things and in recent years we often hear that it means to "be in awe of" God. In this scripture, as with many in the New Testament, the word "be afraid" in verse 4, and "fear" in verse 5, is the same. The

Greek word is "phobethete", which means to be afraid of, terrified, or dread. This is where we get the anglicised word "phobia" from. In past generations, before the 1950s and '60s in the UK, the term more commonly used for the fear of the Lord was "the terror of the Lord".

Undeniably, in the context that Jesus is teaching, He means for His disciples to have a fear and terror of God because He has the power to kill them and throw them into hell. The simple truth of the matter is this; if people get on the wrong side of God, they will experience His terrifying wrath and anger, but if people are right with God, they experience His unfailing love and faithfulness. However, just because some people may be followers of Jesus does not exempt them from the terror of the Lord, as Jesus told His closest followers to also fear God.

We will study this further in the next chapter, but it is important to recognise that because of God's holy nature, His hatred of sin, and His power to throw people into hell, we have the fear of the Lord.

Chapter 8
What Does This Mean For The Believer?

One might think, "Well I understand His wrath is coming on the wicked, but I am saved so I don't need to grapple with this wrathful side of God." Let me start by saying this: an evangelist would entirely disagree! Unless you have the revelation of God's wrath and eternal punishment in hell for the unrepentant sinner, how can you reach out for people with utter conviction that they need to repent and turn to Jesus in order to be saved? If there is no fear for the perishing sinner, we are deluded and lacking zeal in our evangelism. Apostle Paul wrote in 2 Corinthians 5:11, *"Since, then, we know what it is to fear the Lord, we try to persuade others."* Jesus preached more on hell than anyone else recorded in Scripture, I believe as a warning to escape it.

If we cannot grasp the terror of being on the wrong side of God on that day of judgement, then do we really expect to have the same urgency as Jesus, the Apostles and the early church to preach the Gospel that can save them? For the Gospel is the power of God unto salvation (Romans 1:16). One considerable sign of a lack of the fear of the Lord in the Church today is a lack of preaching on hell and the wrath of God. Often when it might be mentioned in a sermon though, we can flutter over it, to try and prevent people from going into fear! We should be trying to bring people into a holy fear rather than "protect" them from it!

How far-fetched it may seem today for people to come to a Church and be gripped in fear of the judgement of God. But when you look at the revivals over the centuries, this is what has happened! David and Patricia Knowles write that a revival is "a time when Christians and unbelievers are struck with the reality and power of the tangible presence of God, resulting in deep conviction of sin and the fear of the Lord."[1] These great awakenings produced the fruit of right-living as people had been awe-struck, prostrated on the floor, crying out to the Lord Jesus to have mercy on them, and gripped with a holy fear that *"Not everyone who says to me, 'Lord, Lord,' will enter the kingdom of heaven."* (Matthew 7:21)

Why are we afraid to be preaching like Jesus did? Perhaps it is because we fear what man would think, more than we fear God! I hope that more people come to our churches with a holy fear of God's judgement, because then we can preach the Gospel and lead them to true repentance and life-saving discipleship.

Another very important consideration for why Christians should fear God is because we are subject to His discipline. Derek Prince writes "It is important for all of us to remember that God's *forgiveness* does not necessarily cancel all the *consequences* of our sins."[2]

Consider Ananias and Sapphira, spoken of in Acts 5. They were believers and followers of Jesus and members of the Church, but their actions of lying to the Holy Spirit and conspiring to test the Spirit caused their immediate death (5:4, 9). Fact: **Christians can face severe**

---

[1] *'Keys to Revival Praying'*, by David and Patricia Knowles, page 9
[2] https://www.derekprince.com/teaching/97-4

and immediate consequences for their sin. Now either this makes you tremble in a holy fear of Christ's judgement and discipline (like it did in Acts 5:5,11) or you choose to somehow disregard the warning of how God can act in such circumstances.

Consider also Jesus' warning to the seven churches, recorded in Revelation chapters 2 and 3. Jesus speaks to several of these churches, acknowledging the good things they are doing. But to the majority of the churches, Jesus also gives a warning, reprimanding them for what He is not pleased with. Jesus warns with these words, **"But I have this against you"**! Pretty severe words from Jesus! Have you ever heard Jesus say this to you? When Jesus delivers these sombre words to His churches, He then exposes what sin there is and warns them that **"if they do not repent"**, there will be costly consequences delivered by the hand of Jesus Himself:

"If you do not repent, I will come to you and remove your lampstand from its place" (Revelation 2:5)

"Repent therefore! Otherwise, I will soon come to you and will fight against them with the sword of my mouth." (Revelation 2:16)

"I will make those who commit adultery with her [Jezebel] suffer intensely, unless they repent of her ways. I will strike her children dead. Then all the churches will know that I am he who searches hearts and minds, and I will repay each of you according to your deeds." (Revelation 2:22-23)

"Wake up! Strengthen what remains and is about to die, for I have found your deeds unfinished in the sight of my God. Remember, therefore, what you have received and heard; hold it fast, and repent. But if you do not wake up, I will come like a thief, and you will not know at what time I will come to you." (Revelation 3:2-3)

"I know your deeds, that you are neither cold nor hot. I wish you were either one or the other! So, because you are lukewarm—neither hot nor cold—I am about to spit you out of my mouth." (Revelation 3:15-16)

At the end of this, Jesus reminds the Church, *"Those whom I love I rebuke and discipline. So be earnest and repent."* Let us take from this the importance of Christian repentance. Let us not be deceived to think that because Jesus loves us that we do not need to be earnest and repent. Let us repent of our sin, because if we do not, there can be eternal consequences.

There are further examples in Scripture of where there are consequences to the believers for their sin. Jesus warns us that *"every kind of sin and slander can be forgiven, but blasphemy against the Spirit will not be forgiven. Anyone who speaks a word against the Son of Man will be forgiven, but anyone who speaks against the Holy Spirit will not be forgiven, either in this age or in the age to come."* (Matthew 12:31-32). I am terrified when Christians speak against supernatural signs and wonders so quickly, claiming them to be demonic! Please, I beg you, be so cautious of saying such things, for we do not want to call something that is the Holy Spirit, evil. Have the fear of God in your words!

Furthermore, in Matthew 12:36-37, Jesus says, *"But I tell you that everyone will have to give account on the day of judgment for every empty word they have spoken. For by your words you will be acquitted, and by your words you will be condemned."*

Also, the Apostle John says, *"If you see a fellow believer sinning in a way that does not lead to death, you should pray, and God will give that person life. But there is a sin that leads to death, and I am not saying you should pray for those who commit it."* (1 John 5:16)

God disciplines those He loves, and those He calls His children (Hebrews 12:6). So even when we endure the Lord's chastisement against us, we can hold on to His love and faithfulness towards us, but this should not make us assume that we do not need to humbly repent when we do sin because we know that there can be eternal consequences.

The fear of the Lord keeps the believer from sinning and leads us into holiness

The Bible warns us not to treat God's discipline lightly – scoffing at it or putting it to one side (Hebrews 12:5). We should fear His discipline because nobody wants to feel the weight of a Father's discipline, for "it is never pleasant at the time". We would surely work hard to avoid sin to prevent us from being disciplined for our bad behaviour and instead, have a desire to please our Heavenly Father and bring Him joy.

As we explain in Chapter 6, what is our attitude towards realising we can be doing something that God absolutely hates? I hate seeing my children fight each other; it fills me with a righteous anger. I hate the sin of siblings quarrelling. But so does God, and in fact God hates that sin a lot more than I do. Proverbs 6 describes a list of seven sins that God hates, but the seventh sin (causing discord amongst the brethren) is an abomination. So when I am aware that I can do something that God hates and that He may inflict consequences on me for my actions, that gives me a holy fear of Him. I don't want to sin, so the fear of the Lord keeps me from sinning.

What we are talking about is the believer's sanctification; the journey of denying our sinful nature and walking in more holiness. As believers it is our primary function in Christ to be made holy:

Colossians 1:22 *"But now he has reconciled you by Christ's physical body through death to present you holy in his sight, without blemish and free from accusation."*

Ephesians 1:4 *"For he chose us in him before the creation of the world to be holy and blameless in his sight."*

Ezekiel 43:12 *"And this is the basic law of the Temple: absolute holiness! The entire top of the mountain where the Temple is built is holy. Yes, this is the basic law of the Temple."*

Holiness is not only the basic law of the Church and our perfect final state, but also foundational to our personal relationship with the Lord, *"for those who are not holy will not see the Lord."* (Hebrews 12:14b)

Now this true pursuit of holiness and consecration of oneself can only be done with the fear of the Lord. In fact, as we pursue holiness, we must go in the way of the fear of the Lord. Other pursuits of holiness may not prosper; it is in the fear of the Lord in which we come into perfect Christian holiness. 2 Corinthians 6 speaks about not being equally yoked with unbelievers and exhorts us to holiness because we are God's people and children. In verse 17, Paul quotes Isaiah 52:11, *"Come out from them and be separate, says the Lord. Touch no unclean thing, and I will receive you."*

2 Corinthians 7 then starts with these encouraging words, *"Therefore, beloved, since we have these promises, let us cleanse ourselves from everything that defiles body and spirit, perfecting holiness in the fear of God."* The ESV version equally says, *"bringing holiness to completion in the fear of God."*

If we are wanting to be holy unto the Lord and reach something of a Christian "perfection", or "completion" in holiness, it must be done *in the fear of God*! The fear of the Lord is the path in which we walk towards holiness; it is a good thing, and absolutely necessary for the believer! We are told in Philippians 2:12, *"Therefore, my dear friends, as you have always obeyed—not only in my presence, but now much more in my absence—continue to work out your salvation with fear and trembling"*. This "working out of your salvation" is your sanctification; becoming more like Christ and again is to be done on the path of holy fear and trembling.

Once the Christian is saved in Christ, we are to pursue the path of sanctification. But "upward" is not the only path one can take as a believer. It is also possible to fall away again. 2 Peter 3:17 states, *"Therefore, dear friends, since you have been forewarned, be on your guard so that you may not be carried away by the error of the lawless and fall from your secure position."* Likewise, in Galatians 5:4, *"You who are trying to be justified by the law have been severed from Christ; you have fallen away from grace."* Also in 1 Corinthians 10:12, *"So the one who thinks he is standing firm should be careful not to fall."*

Consider Romans 11:17-22. Paul is writing to the Gentile believers in Rome, trying to persuade them to share his heart for the Jewish people.

"If some of the branches have been broken off, and you, though a wild olive shoot, have been grafted in among the others and now share in the nourishing sap from the olive root, do not consider yourself to be superior to those other branches. If you do, consider this: You do not support the root, but the root supports you. You will say then, 'Branches were broken off so that I could be grafted in.' Granted. But they were broken off because of unbelief, and you stand by faith. **Do not be arrogant, but tremble. For if God did not spare the natural branches, he will not spare you either.**

Consider therefore the kindness and sternness of God: sternness to those who fell, but kindness to you, **provided that you continue in his kindness. Otherwise, you also will be cut off."**

I consider this such an important reality: It is possible for the believer to be cut off and separated from Christ. We can all fall!

I encourage the reader to go through these passages prayerfully to consider this point.

Hebrews 6:4-8 *"It is impossible for those who have once been enlightened, who have tasted the heavenly gift, who have shared in the Holy Spirit, who have tasted the goodness of the word of God and the powers of the coming age and who have fallen away, to be brought back to repentance. To their loss they are crucifying the Son of God all over again and subjecting him to public disgrace. Land that drinks in the rain often falling on it and that produces a crop useful to those for whom it is farmed receives the blessing of God. But land that produces thorns and thistles is worthless and is in danger of being cursed. In the end it will be burned."*

Hebrews 10:26-31 *"If we deliberately keep on sinning after we have received the knowledge of the truth, no sacrifice for sins is left, but only a fearful expectation of judgment and of raging fire that will consume the enemies of God. Anyone who rejected the law of Moses died without mercy on the testimony of two or three witnesses. How much more severely do you think someone deserves to be punished who has trampled the Son of God underfoot, who has treated as an unholy thing the blood of the covenant that sanctified them, and who has insulted the Spirit of grace? For we know him who said, "It is mine to avenge; I will repay," and again, "The Lord will judge his people." It is a dreadful thing to fall into the hands of the living God."*

Hebrews 12:25 *"See to it that you do not refuse him who speaks. If they did not escape when they refused him who warned them on earth, how much less will we, if we turn away from him who warns us from heaven?"*

2 Peter 2:20-22 *"And when people escape from the wickedness of the world by knowing our Lord and Savior Jesus Christ and then get tangled up and* *enslaved by sin again, they are worse off than before. It would be better if they had never known the way to righteousness than to know it and then reject the command they were given to live a holy life. They prove the truth of this proverb: 'A dog returns to its vomit.' And another says, 'A washed pig returns to the mud.'"*

Consider this Scripture again:

"It would be better if they had never known the way to righteousness than to know it and then reject the command they were given to live a holy life."

We have been given the command to live a holy life! The fear of God, His holiness and justice, particularly for those who were once saved by grace to then walk away and reject Him, should compel us to take this seriously for ourselves and for others. None of us are exempt from this warning, and so cry out to God, in holy fear, to have mercy for you and for loved ones. Dear Christian, "work out your salvation in fear and trembling"! We are all in total need of His grace; "Help me Lord to never fall away", and God will give you grace. But God gives grace to the humble, whilst opposing the proud. In the fear of God, people are driven to eagerly pursue humility, holiness, honesty, and right living.

Chapter 9
Key To Obedience

"'Don't lay a hand on the boy!' the angel said. 'Do not hurt him in any way, for now I know that you truly fear God. You have not withheld from me even your son, your only son.'" (Genesis 22:1)

Many of the saints have been tested by the Lord, and their obedience to God's word has been underpinned by their fear of Him. "Now I know that you truly fear God."

When we consider the previous chapter: that as believers there can be consequences for our sin, God can be displeased with our actions, and none are exempt from falling from grace, this gives us a holy fear that drives us to want to obey Him and be faithful to Him. The fear of the Lord is key to Christian obedience and faithful living.

As previously mentioned, the fear of the Lord produces a hatred of evil in us and motivates us to keep away from sin. **When we hate evil and are motivated to stay away from sin, then the path of obedience is set before us.** There is nowhere else to turn! This is why the fear of the Lord does not make us want to run *away* from God and His ways, but it makes us want to run *to* God and His ways. The fear of God's hatred of evil and the consequence of sin makes us cry out to God for holiness. *"Teach me your way, O LORD, that I may walk in your truth;*

unite my heart to fear your name" (Psalm 86:11, ESV). *"See if there is any offensive way in me, and lead me in the way everlasting."* (Psalm 139:24)

The fear of the Lord helps us to earnestly seek Him and desire for His Spirit and His ways to rule in our lives. We must be aware that we can do things that please the Holy Spirit or grieve the Holy Spirit:

Ephesians 4:30 *"Do not grieve the Holy Spirit of God, with whom you were sealed for the day of redemption".*

Galatians 6:7-9 *"Do not be deceived: God cannot be mocked. A man reaps what he sows. Whoever sows to please their flesh, from the flesh will reap destruction; whoever sows to **please the Spirit**, from the Spirit will reap eternal life. Let us not become weary in doing good, for at the proper time we will reap a harvest if we do not give up."*

Obedience is a foundational part of our faith in Jesus and we must have the right attitude towards it.

Consider these 3 scriptures on obedience:

Luke 8:21 *"Jesus replied, 'My mother and my brothers are all those who hear God's word and obey it.'"*

James 1:22 *"But don't just listen to God's word. You must do what it says. Otherwise, you are only fooling yourselves."*

Philippians 2:12-13 *"Dear friends, you always followed my instructions when I was with you. And now that I am away, it is even more important. Work hard to show the results of your salvation, obeying God with deep reverence and fear. For God is working in you, giving you the desire and the power to do what pleases him."*

Let me share a time with you when I was **not** obedient to God's command, and I chose not to fear Him. Since walking with the Lord, regular and long times of fasting was a spiritual discipline I had. I had the discipline for years. At one point I grew too presumptuous that God would give me grace to do long fasts, and for the first time I broke a fast due to an anxiety for my health. This put a stumbling block in me, and I resisted doing longer fasts for months, and then years. During this time, I continuously felt convicted that I should return to the godly discipline of fasting, but I never truly did. This was a sign that I was not fearing the Lord, of which I now repent. The Lord impressed on me more and more that He wanted me to do it, but I tried to close my ears to it, because truth be told – I didn't want to fast!

Eventually there came a point where the Lord spoke such a strong word of encouragement and direction to me to return to fasting for longer periods of time. I responded with a joyful, "yes" and I was convinced that I would indeed do so, until I realised weeks then passed without me showing any signs of fasting as I just really wanted to enjoy a few more weeks without doing it! The issue again, is that I did not fear God. I was deluded into thinking, "It's ok, the Lord has mercy and grace for me. He understands my weaknesses and I'm sure it's fine to not do it anyway. I'll get back to it one day." My view of Jesus became distorted into thinking that His grace for me would protect me from His discipline, even though I knew I was being disobedient. How wrong of me! Shortly afterwards I was listening to a talk when the speaker mentioned some pretty extreme fasts that the Lord had asked her to do, and she was **obedient**! Like a download of information and with a deep conviction of my sin, the Lord instructed me to do over 20 fasts that were each a longer length than any fast I had done in years and told me to finish the 20+ fasts by the end of the year. This came with a weighty warning, and I knew this was the Lord's discipline and a consequence to past rebellion from fasting. I cannot explain the weight of warning that this came with. I realised I had treated the Lord's commands lightly and that He had been VERY gracious to me. In the fear of God, I **DO NOT** want to test His patience like that again! Lord, help me!

God's intentions in discipline are good but it's never enjoyable at the time (Hebrews 12:11). During that time, I had to seek the fear of the Lord again. I had to change my mind to focus on the fact that He's not just a nice friend who's suggesting I fast, it's the LORD who's commanding me to! I learnt in this time that the fear of the Lord helps us to obey the Lord **quickly**, and delayed obedience is in fact **disobedience** and a sign that there is a lack of the fear of the Lord! Let us not test His patience or provoke Him to anger (1 Corinthians 10:9).

Part 3

The Fear Of The Lord In The Last Days

Having considered Parts 1 & 2, let us take our focus onto the specific theme of the importance of the fear of the Lord in the last days and the return of Christ.

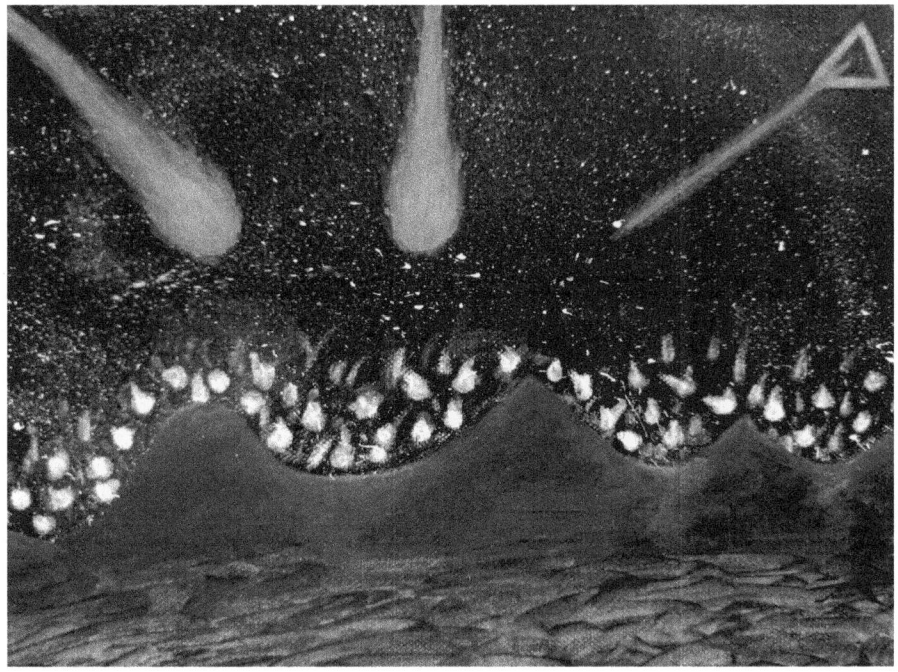

Painting by Bronia Coulshaw: "Tristan's dream of the last days"

Chapter 10
A Dream

In October 2019, I had a dream. For the previous couple of months or so, my wife and I were on a journey of growing more in the fear of the Lord. It was in this season of searching for insight and understanding that I had this dream. In my dream it was night, and in the distance there were a range of mountains. I was amongst a group of people when suddenly on the horizon we saw the most incredible lightning storm. Up to 60 flashes per moment, each one was like a ball of lightning 2-3 times the size of the full moon. I had no idea what it was and so I prayed that it would stop in Jesus' Name. It did not stop, and I knew then that this was from the Lord.

Then came balls of fire hurtling down from the sky, and finally a small triangle of fire, and out of this triangle of fire flowed a river of fire. When I saw this triangle, I exclaimed, "What is that?" The people were fleeing in a mad panic and rushed off into nearby tents. We knew it was the time of God's judgement on the earth. My wife was with me and ran into the tents to tell them about Jesus and to repent. I stood outside the tents watching people hiding under whatever seemed best and said to myself, "It is too late" and then I woke up.

I woke up and saw that the time was 5:05 in the morning. But I did not see 5:05 but read it as SOS (Save Our Souls). "That's fitting!", I thought to myself.

I knew God had spoken and I asked for confirmation of this dream in my daily Bible reading that morning. My daily reading was Psalm 97:1-5,

> *"The Lord is king!*
> *Let the earth rejoice!*
> *Let the farthest coastlands be glad.*
> *Dark clouds surround him.*
> *Righteousness and justice are the foundation of his throne.*
> ***Fire spreads ahead of him***
> *and burns up all his foes.*
> ***His lightning flashes out across the world.***
> *The earth sees and trembles.*
> *The mountains melt like wax before the Lord,*
> *before the Lord of all the earth."*

I knew that this was a dream from the Lord and He had revealed to me something of the coming Day of the Lord and His judgement coming onto the earth. I carry within me the fear of the Lord and I have seen something of the coming judgement of God.

There is one final point to this dream, and that is the triangle of fire with a river of fire flowing out from it. I always wondered if the triangle represented God (sign of the trinity), but I hadn't been given the insight from the Lord yet. It was about 3 years later that I came into understanding of what this was, when I read Daniel 7:9-10,

> *"As I continued to watch,*
> *thrones were set in place,*
> *and the Ancient of Days took His seat.*
> *His clothing was white as snow,*
> *and the hair of His head was like pure wool.*
> ***His throne was flaming with fire,***
> ***and its wheels were all ablaze.***
> ***A river of fire was flowing,***
> ***coming out from His presence.***
> *Thousands upon thousands attended Him,*
> *and myriads upon myriads stood before Him.*
> *The court was convened,*
> *and the books were opened."*

I believe what I saw that night in my dream was something of the Ancient of Days, His throne of flaming fire, and the river of fire flowing out of His presence as His judgement was coming.

That passage in Daniel 7, as well as Psalm 97, are both prophetic of the last days, the return of Christ. When we are aware and in tune with what God does in those days, we will grow in the fear of the Lord. I believe that as we near the last days, the fear of the Lord will be much more evident in God's holy Church and so this message of the fear of the Lord is also a prophetic heralding.

Chapter 11
A Prophetic Message

As we near the return of Christ and are either living in, or drawing near to the last days, there will be an increased recognition of the importance of the fear of the Lord. In Malachi 3:16-18, it is written:

Then those who feared the Lord spoke with each other, and the Lord listened to what they said. In his presence, a scroll of remembrance was written to record the names of those who feared him and always thought about the honour of his name.

"They will be my people," says the Lord of Heaven's Armies. "On the day when I act in judgement, they will be my own special treasure. I will spare them as a father spares an obedient child. Then you will again see the difference between the righteous and the wicked, between those who serve God and those who do not."

In the last days there will be a coming together of those who fear the Lord and a recognition in the courts of heaven of who these people are. The Lord then goes on to say that there will be a noticeable difference between the righteous and the wicked. This noticeable difference between the righteous and the wicked is important to grasp. Jesus warns that in the last days there will be an increase of wickedness (Matthew 24:12), but also that the Church will be set-apart, ready for the Bridegroom's return (Revelation 19:7-8). But the point to note is that as we near the day of the Lord's return, we will begin to see a greater distinction between the people of God and the people of the world. Indeed, there will be a great separation, and a significant mark that God's people will have that will distinguish them is that they will fear the Lord. This is also noted in scriptures such as Revelation 11:18, 14:7, 19:5.

As we near the day of the Lord's judgement on the earth we must ensure that we are marked as the holy people of God, set-apart from this world, eagerly awaiting the Bridegroom's return, and fearing the Lord. The more we have our eyes fixed on the return of Jesus and the coming of the Kingdom, the more prepared we will be for it. Therefore, it is helpful to meditate regularly on the return of Christ so that we are not left unaware and *"asleep"* as this day nears.

In this next section we will explore some basic principles and truths of the last days and the return of Christ to help guide us. This is vital to do, as so much of our motivation for godly living comes from our ***awareness*** of Christ's return.

Chapter 12
The Return Of The King And His Coming Judgement

"Blow the trumpet in Zion; sound the alarm on my holy hill. Let all who live in the land tremble, for the day of the LORD is coming." Joel 2:1

These are some basic facts of the return of Jesus Christ that are helpful to consider:

Jesus will return to the earth in bodily form. *"'Men of Galilee,' they said, 'why do you stand here looking into the sky? This same Jesus, who has been taken from you into heaven, will come back in the same way you have seen him go into heaven.'"* (Acts 1:11)

The whole world will see Him. *"So if anyone tells you, 'There he is, out in the wilderness,' do not go out; or, 'Here he is, in the inner rooms,' do not believe it. For as lightning that comes from the east is visible even in the west, so will be the coming of the Son of Man."* (Matthew 24:26-27)

"'Look, he is coming with the clouds,' and 'every eye will see him, even those who pierced him'; and all peoples on earth 'will mourn because of him.' So shall it be! Amen." (Revelation 1:7)

Jesus's second coming will be in great power and glory, and He will reign as King on the earth. *"Then will appear the sign of the Son of Man in heaven. And then all the peoples of the earth will mourn when they see the Son of Man coming on the clouds of heaven, with power and great glory."* (Matthew 24:30)

"When the Son of Man comes in his glory, and all the angels with him, he will sit on his glorious throne." (Matthew 25:31)

Jesus will come for the salvation of the Universal Church and the dead in Christ will rise from the dead. *"So Christ was sacrificed once to take away the sins of many; and he will appear a second time, not to bear sin, but to bring salvation to those who are eagerly waiting for him".* (Hebrews 9:28)

"For the Lord himself will come down from heaven with a commanding shout, with the voice of the archangel, and with the trumpet call of God. First, the believers who have died will rise from their graves. Then, together with them, we who are still alive and remain on the earth will be caught up in the clouds to meet the Lord in the air. Then we will be with the Lord forever. So encourage each other with these words." (1 Thessalonians 4:16-18)

Jesus will come to judge the wicked. *"In flaming fire, [Jesus will] bring judgment on those who don't know God and on those who refuse to obey the Gospel of our Lord Jesus."* (2 Thessalonians 1:8)

"For the Son of Man will come with his angels in the glory of his Father and will judge all people according to what they have done." (Matthew 16:27)

Furthermore, the last time Jesus arrived in Jerusalem He was riding humbly on a colt as the Saviour of the world. The next time Jesus rides into Jerusalem, He will be riding on a horse of war as the judge of the whole earth.

"I saw heaven standing open and there before me was a white horse, whose rider is called Faithful and True. With justice he judges and wages war. His eyes are like blazing fire, and on his head are many crowns. He has a name written on him that no one knows but he himself. He is dressed in a robe dipped in blood, and his name is the Word of God. The armies of heaven were following him, riding on white horses and dressed in fine linen, white and clean. Coming out of his mouth is a sharp sword with which to strike down the nations. 'He will rule them with an iron sceptre.' He treads the winepress of the fury of the wrath of God Almighty. On his robe and on his thigh he has this name written:

King of kings and Lord of lords."

Jesus will be coming in wrath and justice. It will be too late for repentance, no more time for mercy, but it will be the time for judgement. *"As the weeds are pulled up and burned in the fire, so it will be at the end of the age. The Son of Man will send out his angels, and they will weed out of his kingdom everything that causes sin and all who do evil. They will throw them into the blazing furnace, where there will be weeping and gnashing of teeth."* (Matthew 13:40-42)

For many Christians, we know this in our minds, but do we really relate to this side of Jesus? Do we connect with this side of Jesus and long for His return? If some of us are honest, we may even be thinking, "I don't like what I read about Jesus here." Whereas others may be thinking "I don't connect with this side of Jesus at all." Remember here, that the encouragement of having the fear of the Lord is to know God better and have deeper intimacy with Him.

In the context of the day of the Lord and His coming judgement, 2 Peter 3:11-12 says, "Since everything will be destroyed in this way, what kind of people ought you to be? You ought to **live *holy* and *godly* lives** as you look forward to the day of God and speed its coming. That day will bring about the destruction of the heavens by fire, and the elements will melt in the heat." Then in verse 14, "So then, dear friends, since you are looking forward to this, make every effort to be found spotless, blameless and at peace with him."

This is a call to the believers, that as we become aware of God's coming judgement our godly response and motivation is to live holy, godly, pure and blameless lives. We need to be motivated, not "put-off" from meditating on the scriptures around Christ's judgement and His return, because the result of a greater awareness and revelation of this will bring a fear of God that purifies the bride of Christ.

At the coming of the King and His Kingdom, this judgement and vengeance will come. A simple study on the Parables of Jesus reveals this. In Matthew's Gospel, Jesus says again and again, "The Kingdom of God is like...." and then goes on to say about His return and the judgement of the wicked. For example:

Parable of The Net - Matthew 13:47-50

"Once again, the kingdom of heaven is like a net that was let down into the lake and caught all kinds of fish. When it was full, the fishermen pulled it up on the shore. Then they sat down and collected the good fish in baskets, but threw the bad away. This is how it will be at the end of the age. The angels will come and separate the wicked from the righteous and throw them into the blazing furnace, where there will be weeping and gnashing of teeth."

In your own time you can read the following parables in Appendix 1 which shares the same message.

- Parable of The Weeds Among the Wheat - Matthew 13:24-30

- Parable of The Unforgiving Servant - Matthew 18:23-35
- Parable of the Marriage Feast - Matthew 22:1-14
- Parable of Faithful vs. Wicked Servant - Matthew 24:45-51
- Parable of The Ten Virgins - Matthew 25:1-13
- Parable of Ten Talents - Matthew 25:14-30

Chapter 13
What About The Believer's Judgement?

We know that all Christians will be judged by Jesus Christ, once He has returned. (2 Corinthians 5:10) We also know that we will be judged for our works, both good and bad. But what does this mean?

1 Corinthians 3:12-15 gives us good insight into the believers' judgement. *Anyone who builds on that foundation may use a variety of materials—gold, silver, jewels, wood, hay, or straw. But on the judgment day, fire will reveal what kind of work each builder has done. The fire will show if a person's work has any value. If the work survives, that builder will receive a reward. But if the work is burned up, the builder will suffer great loss. The builder will be saved, but like someone barely escaping through a wall of flames.*

When we come before the judgement seat of Christ, it will be a reward-giving ceremony. The Greek word for the believer's judgement is "Bema" which has similar attributes to the Olympic prize giving ceremony.

This passage shows that our works of service that we accomplish in this life on earth can either be gold, silver, rubies, wood, hay or straw. And when we are judged, we will be judged for our works, both good and bad. "Fire will reveal what kind of work each builder has done." (1 Corinthians 3:13)

Under the fire of Christ's judgement, all works of service that believers have done that are wood, hay or straw will be burned up in the fire. There will be no reward for these things and the builder will suffer great loss. But all work of gold, silver or rubies will survive the fire and the worker will receive an award that blesses the King. Something to note here is that we see God values the *quality* of a worker's service, more than the *quantity*.

Derek Prince[3] shares some helpful insight into how we may test if our works are of eternal value or burned up in the fire:

1) Is it in obedience to God's word?
2) Are your motives godly?
3) Are you doing it in the Spirit's power or in the flesh?

We can see further, how Jesus expresses the reality of the believer's judgement of works through the parable of ten talents (Matthew 25:14-30)

> *"Again, it will be like a man going on a journey, who called his servants and entrusted his wealth to them. To one he gave five bags of gold, to another two bags, and to another one bag, each according to his ability. Then he went on his journey. The man who had received five bags of gold went at once and put his money to work and gained five bags more. So also, the one with two bags of gold gained two more. But the man who had received one bag went off, dug a hole in the ground and hid his master's money."*

---

[3] *'Foundations for Christian Living'*, by Derek Prince, DPM International, page 494.

"After a long time the master of those servants returned and settled accounts with them. The man who had received five bags of gold brought the other five. 'Master,' he said, 'you entrusted me with five bags of gold. See, I have gained five more.'

"His master replied, 'Well done, good and faithful servant! You have been faithful with a few things; I will put you in charge of many things. Come and share your master's happiness!'

"The man with two bags of gold also came. 'Master,' he said, 'you entrusted me with two bags of gold; see, I have gained two more.'

"His master replied, 'Well done, good and faithful servant! You have been faithful with a few things; I will put you in charge of many things. Come and share your master's happiness!'

"Then the man who had received one bag of gold came. 'Master,' he said, 'I knew that you are a hard man, harvesting where you have not sown and gathering where you have not scattered seed. So I was afraid and went out and hid your gold in the ground. See, here is what belongs to you.'

"His master replied, 'You wicked, lazy servant! So you knew that I harvest where I have not sown and gather where I have not scattered seed? Well then, you should have put my money on deposit with the bankers, so that when I returned I would have received it back with interest.

"'So take the bag of gold from him and give it to the one who has ten bags. For whoever has will be given more, and they will have an abundance. Whoever does not have, even what they have will be taken from them. And throw that worthless servant outside, into the darkness, where there will be weeping and gnashing of teeth.'

Note that all three were the Master's servants who knew Him and were in relationship with Him. But under the Bema seat of judgement, we will be judged for our works, both good and bad. The first two servants, though they had different amounts of grace, doubled their gifts that they were given by the Master; they were fruitful and were both accepted by the Master as "Good and faithful servants".

The third servant, however, failed to increase his talent (produce fruit for the Kingdom). He was judged harshly and was called "a wicked and lazy servant". His sentence was severe; *"throw that worthless servant outside, into the darkness, where there will be weeping and gnashing of teeth."*

Our *faithfulness* as servants of Christ is judged by whether or not we are fruitful. If we walk through the Christian life and are not fruitful for the Kingdom it means that we are unfaithful. Faithfulness on judgement day is not based on our belief in Christ, but our obedience to do the work God has given us to do. **We must ask ourselves, "What am I doing for the Lord with what He has given me?", "Am I aware of what the Spirit is leading me into?"**

A holy fear of the believer's judgement should move us to eagerly seek the Lord as to what work He has called us to do. When we know the work He calls us to do (and it can vary in seasons), then we are to serve Him in fear that we may do the work obediently, with a godly motive, and reliant on His power and grace – otherwise that work might be wood, hay or straw.

Let's not be deceived to think that the believer's judgement will all be about a big party because we are all saved by faith in Jesus. We will be judged for our works and the believer's judgement should strongly motivate us, in trembling fear, to remain true to the faith and obedient to what God calls us to do. 1 Peter 1:17, *"And remember that the heavenly Father to whom you pray has no favourites. He will judge or reward you according to what you do. So you must live in reverent fear of him during your time here as 'temporary residents'."*

As I have already mentioned, as we near the Lord's return the holy fear of not being found to be faithful servants should motivate us to eagerly pursue the Lord, asking Him whether or not we are doing the work He has called us to. Note, that the fear of God is not a bad thing that drives us to work in order to be saved, but instead should motivate us to drive us to His presence, where we seek intimate counsel from Him, hearing His voice and obeying Him.

Consider the parable of the faithful servant in Matthew 24:42-51. Jesus is explicitly talking about the end times and His return, and He warns His hearers that when the Son of Man returns, you need to be ready!

"So you, too, must keep watch! For you don't know what day your Lord is coming. Understand this: If a homeowner knew exactly when a burglar was coming, he would keep watch and not permit his house to be broken into. You also must be ready all the time, for the Son of Man will come when least expected.

"A faithful, sensible servant is one to whom the master can give the responsibility of managing his other household servants and feeding them. If the master returns and finds that the servant has done a good job, there will be a reward. I tell you the truth, the master will put that servant in charge of all he owns. But what if the servant is evil and thinks, 'My master won't be back for a while,' and he begins beating the other servants, partying, and getting drunk? The master will return unannounced and unexpected, and he will cut the servant to pieces and assign him a place with the hypocrites. In that place there will be weeping and gnashing of teeth.

Ask yourselves, are you being faithful with the people the Lord has given you to care after? Are you diverting away from the true call of God by enjoying earthly pleasures instead? The judge stands at the door – be faithful servants of the Lord to the very end. For he who endures to the end will be saved (Matthew 24:13).

As we have spoken, much of the attention of the Lord's return is the coming judgement, for the believer and unbeliever and this should awaken us to a holy fear of the Lord. It is also helpful to consider some of the realities of what will happen in the last days, as this will show us again, the importance of standing firm in the last days, in the fear of the Lord.

Chapter 14
What Will Happen In The Last Days?

Jesus spoke about the signs of His coming, I believe, as a warning to the Church. These warnings were given in order to *protect* His sheep from the evil that is to come. If we do not take note of these prophetic warnings from Jesus, we are at risk of straying away from the Lord and His holy ways. Proverbs 29:13 warns us "Where there is no prophetic vision the people cast off restraint", in other words they **run wild!** Let us not be ignorant or asleep to the reality of the signs of the last days and let us prepare accordingly.

The signs of His coming

Jesus tells us of different signs in different places. I have found it helpful to put these signs into four categories that David Pawson[4] had written on:

1) **There will be signs on the earth:** Wars and rumours of wars, earthquakes and famines (Matthew 24:6-7)

---

[4] *When Jesus Returns*, by David Pawson, pages 22/24/27

2) **There will be signs in the Church:**

   1. "There will be an increase of sin and wickedness (Matthew 24:12, 2 Timothy 3:1-5).

   2. There will be an increase of deception, through false prophets and teachers (Matthew 24:4-5 & 24)

   3. There will be an increase of persecution for the believers (Luke 21:12, 16-17)

   4. Many will leave the faith (Matthew 24:10)

   5. The love of many will grow cold (Matthew 24:12, 2 Timothy 3:1 & 4)

3) **There will be signs in the Middle East/Israel:** The 'abomination that causes desolation' and ultimate blasphemy, a man or idol standing in the holy place of the Temple in Jerusalem. This will be the time of the "Great suffering/ tribulation of Israel". (Matthew 24:15, Daniel 11:31-32)

4) **There will be signs in the sky:** The sun will be dark, the moon won't shine, stars will fall from the sky and the heavenly bodies shaken. (Matthew 24:29)

The signs that we will focus on in this chapter are signs in the Church as these are signs manifested in people, rather than on the earth or in the sky.

These signs in the Church are clear warnings from the Lord, as they all express the increase of evil in the last days. Some Christians believe that the world will become a better place the nearer we approach the Lord's return, but this is not what Jesus has said. Even though there will be great moves of God in these days as the Gospel is preached throughout the whole world and the Church awakens and looks up towards our redemption, there are still these solemn warnings that can be summed up in a conclusion like this:

In the last days there will be very difficult times. Not just 'some', but MANY will leave the faith. There will be an increase of sin and wickedness and the love of many will grow cold. Many will be deceived by false teachings and false prophets, and God's people will suffer increased persecution.

Jesus is expressing the importance about not straying away from the faith and to ensure to live holy lives and walk in the truth.

In light of the warnings that Jesus gives the Church, what 'take home' points do we need to be aware of and how does the fear of God help?

1: There will be an increase of sin and wickedness. We must have a holy hatred towards sin and keep ourselves from sin. *"By fearing the Lord, people avoid evil."* (Proverbs 16:6) We must be able to discern rightly between wickedness and godliness, and for that you need the Holy Spirit and conviction of the Scriptures. *"Therefore, beloved, since we have these promises, let us cleanse ourselves from everything that defiles body and spirit, perfecting holiness in the fear of God."* (2 Corinthians 7:1)

2: There will be an increase of deception, through false prophets and teachers. To help guard ourselves from false teachers we must have godly wisdom and knowledge of the truth. *"The fear of the Lord teaches wisdom."* (Proverbs 15:33). To help protect us from falling into deceptive teaching ourselves, we should consider James 3:1, *"Not many of you should become teachers, my fellow believers, because you know that we who teach will be judged more strictly."*

3: There will be an increase of persecution for the believers. We must be sure to never deny Christ, even in the midst of persecution, for we know what it means to fear God and are aware that at judgement, *"If we deny Christ, He will deny us."* (2 Timothy 2:12)

4: Many will leave the faith. We must know the covenant faithfulness of God and know the consequences of those who leave the faith. *"If we disown Christ, Christ will disown us"* (2 Timothy 2:12)

5: The love of many will grow cold. We must persevere in love. *"Take notice, therefore, of the kindness and severity of God: severity to those who fell, but kindness to you, **IF you continue in His kindness.** Otherwise you also will be cut off"* (Romans 11:22). We must pursue forgiving love for each other. *"In anger his master handed him over to the jailers to be tortured, until he should pay back all he owed. 'This is how my heavenly Father will treat each of you unless you forgive your brother or sister from your heart.'"* (Matthew 18:34-35)

These 'take home' points are very simple but give us insight into what will be required of us to endure the last days; holiness, wisdom, patient perseverance, loyalty even to the death, and love. Hence in the last days there will be a growing importance for the believers to have the fear of the Lord.

Part 4

Practical Outworking

Chapter 15
A Daily Sign Of The Fear Of The Lord

Let us consider in this fourth and final part of the book, what it can look like to practically live in the fear of the Lord in normal day to day lives.

In Psalm 34:11-14 it is written,

"Come, my children, listen to me; I will teach you the fear of the Lord. Whoever of you loves life and desires to see many good days, keep your tongue from evil and your lips from telling lies. Turn from evil and do good; seek peace and pursue it."

Joy Dawson[5] wrote that Psalm 34 is the school of the fear of the Lord, referencing such scriptures as the above . On teaching the fear of the Lord, the psalmist points out, to "keep your tongue from evil and your lips from telling lies." This highlights an incredibly valuable lesson in the teaching of the fear of the Lord; it is not so much about the words that you speak, it is more about the words that you do not speak! What

---

[5] *'Intimate Friendship with God'*, by Joy Dawson, Youth With A Mission, page 126/127

do I mean? A sign of someone who fears the Lord is not so much about the praiseworthy, lovely and holy words that come out of their mouth, it is about the sinful words that **DO NOT** come out of their mouth!

When we have the fear of the Lord and hate what is evil, we will put a guard over our mouth to prevent us from speaking things that God hates. Proverbs 13:3 says, *"He who guards his mouth protects his life, but the one who opens his lips invites his own ruin"*, and we can pray *"Set a guard, O LORD, over my mouth; keep watch at the door of my lips"* (Psalm 141:3). Keeping a guard over our mouths can protect us from evil talk, such as complaining, gossiping, proud talk, course joking, lies, things spoken in revenge, things spoken in fits of anger, divisive, defiling words – the list goes on.

James 3:3-6 speaks of taming the tongue. *"When we put bits into the mouths of horses to make them obey us, we can turn the whole animal. Or take ships as an example. Although they are so large and are driven by strong winds, they are steered by a very small rudder wherever the pilot wants to go. Likewise, the tongue is a small part of the body, but it makes great boasts. Consider what a great forest is set on fire by a small spark. The tongue also is a fire, a world of evil among the parts of the body. It corrupts the whole body, sets the whole course of one's life on fire, and is itself set on fire by hell."*

Jesus also warns us of the consequences of evil talk from our mouths. *"But I tell you that men will give an account on the day of judgment for every careless word they have spoken. For by your words you will be acquitted, and by your words you will be condemned."* (Matthew 12:36-37)

This awareness and holy fear should indeed put a guard over our mouths. If we are tempted to sin by what we say, we know it comes from the heart (Luke 6:45). We need to grow in sanctification in purifying our hearts, but we (even without perfect sanctification of the heart) can *choose* to say "NO" to speaking evil things. I can't tell you how many times the fear of the Lord has helped me shut my mouth from saying what I want to say and am deeply convicted when my tongue gives way. Self-control of the tongue is a highly valuable area to work on in ourselves and by taming the tongue we can become more holy in all areas and get closer to Christian perfection. In James 3:2b it says, *"If anyone is never at fault in what he says, he is a perfect man, able to control his whole body."*

Chapter 16
The Fear Of The Lord In Worship

On a simple level I find it helpful to define "worship" – or at least differentiate it from thanksgiving and praise.

Thanksgiving is being thankful. Thanking God for who He is and what He has done for us and will continue to do for us. *Thanksgiving is a response to God's goodness.*

Praise is expressed in scripture mainly through singing, music, clapping hands, dancing, and lifting hands to the Lord. *Praise is a response to God's greatness.*

Worship is a humble expression of bringing oneself low before God. Most commonly in the Bible it is expressed through bowing or lying prostrate on the ground. The literal term means to kiss the ground between you and the one you are worshipping. *Worship is a response to God's holiness.* When we have revelation of God's holiness, we will have the fear of the Lord and worship Him in an acceptable way, in reverence and godly fear. (Hebrews 12:28).

Matt Redman writes, "Every posture in worship says something of both the worshipper and the one being glorified in. The raising of hands tells of a soul stretched out high in praise and the worth of the one being exalted. Joyful dancing interprets a grateful heart and points in adoration to the source of that joy. When it comes to expressing our worship, what we do on the outside is a key reflection of what's taking place on the inside. Out of the overflow of the heart we speak and sing, we dance and we bow. God reveals, and we respond. God shines, and we reflect. In the very same way, facedown worship is the overflow of a heart humbled and amazed by the glory of God.[6]"

Likewise, Derek Prince writes, "Every word in the Bible, Old Testament and New, that means "worship" is always descriptive of an attitude. Essentially, it is the way we relate to God regarding His holiness." [7]

Whilst we can be thankful to anyone for the good they do in our lives, or give someone praise when they deserve it (Proverbs 31:28-30), or the clapping of hands in applause, worship is totally set apart to God (Exodus 34:14). Therefore, worship is the most intimate expression of admiration that we can give to God. Just as the most intimate part of a marriage, sexual union, is reserved only for your spouse, so also it is with worship to the Lord alone. Worship to God and sexual union in marriage have often been linked together in Scripture, such as Jeremiah's many words condemning Israel for committing adultery against the Lord because they were worshipping idols!

How many of us spend quality, regular time, in worship? Is it a common part of our relationship with God that we humble ourselves and bow low before him? Again, Derek Prince challenges us, "It is easy to question whether any person who has never been on his face before God has ever been very close to God." [8]

---

[6] '*Facedown*', by Matt Redman, page 17
[7] '*Rules of Engagement*', by Derek Prince, Chosen Books, page 67/68
[8] '*Rules of Engagement*', by Derek Prince, Chosen Books, page 68

As worship is the most intimate and set-apart form of admiration and respect to God, this is indeed what the enemy wants of us. Satan ultimately wants our worship. This is what was revealed when Satan tempted Jesus in the wilderness.

When Satan tempted Jesus, looking at Matthew's recording in Chapter 4:8-10, it is written:

"Again, the devil took him to a very high mountain and showed him all the kingdoms of the world and their splendour. 'All this I will give you,' he said, 'if you will bow down and worship me.'

Jesus said to him, 'Away from me, Satan! For it is written: "Worship the Lord your God, and serve him only."'

The scripture Jesus uses to resist the devil is perhaps one of, if not the clearest and most direct scriptures on the point of worshipping God, and that is surely one of the reasons why Jesus would have chosen it. The scripture Jesus is quoting is Deuteronomy 6:13, but in fact the actual Scripture is *"**Fear** the Lord your God and serve him only"*. Jesus, or the New Testament translators, are not wrong in 'misquoting' worship, instead of fear. In fact, Jesus knows what worship really means, it means to fear. You submit to and obey the thing you fear!

The fear of the Lord and worship are totally intertwined. I believe it is like a marriage. It is impossible to truly worship God unless you fear Him, because worship is in recognition and response to God's holiness, His Majesty and Sovereign authority. We are humbled by this reality and therefore throw ourselves down, bowing low on the ground or lying prostrate before Him in holy fear.

This physical act of worship should be empowered and led by the Spirit, and our bodies are to be used in acts of worship. A short look at

Romans 12:1 confirms the same essence of worship, *"I appeal to you therefore, brothers, by the mercies of God, to present your bodies as a living sacrifice, holy and acceptable to God, which is your spiritual worship."* The essence of spiritual worship is to lay our bodies on the alter as a sacrifice – distinguished from praise where one would be dancing and singing, but instead humbly lying down, prostrate, laying our lives down as a sacrifice, in a holy and acceptable way.

Some believers may not have really done this. Some, particularly western, modernistic views of Christianity is to accept Jesus in their life and by doing so "add Him" to their own lives. This is against the Biblical mandate of entering the faith, which is to die to self and rather than Jesus joining you on your life, you deny self by joining Him and following His ways. Jesus says, *"Whoever wants to be my disciple must deny themselves and take up their cross daily and follow me."* (Luke 9:23)

In a similar way, many Christians will lack their worshipful relationship with the Lord. They may be thankful and enjoy times of sung praise but know little about bowing down to worship whether in the physical or spiritual. It is too easy to enjoy the goodness and greatness of God in praise and ignore the holiness of God in worship which is the most intimate form of all. It is a great loss to the Christian who does not regularly enter into this closeness with God, because they refuse to believe, or do not consider that they need to bow to Him. Some may believe that their act of worship is to be spiritual, and not physical too. This denies the concept that the whole spirit, soul and body is to worship God.

But worship is not something to just do because it's "what we should do". It should come as a response to a revelation of who He is. If the reader is not regularly moved by the Spirit to bow down to the Lord in worship, perhaps it's worth doing it as a sign of desire and pray that the Spirit may lead you into His presence in the Holy of Holies.

Once when teaching on the fear of the Lord I encouraged the hearers to come off their seats and spend time with their face to the floor and worship God. One lady scoffed and laughed at the idea but chose to anyway. As she did, she broke down and wept, entering into something of a worshipful intimacy with the Lord that she had never before experienced.

Again, Matt Redman writes, "God is stirring up His church again with a holy urgency to delve deeper into the soul-gripping wonders of who He is. We have heard many new sounds, and we have heard many new songs. But it's time now for a new sense in our songs and sounds. And in the whole of our lives. A sense of wonder. A reverent intimacy, and an intimate reverence. Where friendship underlines fear, and fear underpins friendship. Where rejoicers tremble, and tremblers rejoice. Holy poetry, biblical love songs and anthems of His goodness and greatness. More than anything, the call is for lives lived out in holy obedience and facedown submission – our greatest possible response to the glory of God." [9]

---

[9] *'Facedown'*, by Matt Redman, pages 115/116

Chapter 17
The Fear Of The Lord In Marriage

Now to the important subject of marriage. To those who are not married, please don't skip by this, as many of these truths overflow into the lives of those who are single.

Derek Prince in his book, 'Husbands and Fathers', exhorts the fear of the Lord as the "missing ingredient" to most Christian marriages, and even more so, the "essential ingredient" on which Christian marriage depends. I have a few godly friends who are women, who long for a husband. When they meet a man and begin to tell me about him, and are also open to discernment, my first question is, "Does he fear God?" It is a foundational importance.

Derek Prince continues to write, *"What does all this about the fear of the Lord have to do with the relationship between husbands and wives? I would answer in one word: everything! Out of my own experience in a Christian home, and out of counselling many Christians with problems in their marriages, I have come to a simple conclusion: without the fear of the Lord in both husband and wife, a Christian marriage can never become what God intends it to be..... When a man regulates his relationship with his wife by the all-pervading fear of the Lord, and when his wife responds in the same spirit, their marriage will fulfil the plan of God unfolded in Scripture. Each will bear in mind the awesome responsibility placed on them. The husband by his conduct toward his wife will make it his aim to depict the attitude of Christ toward His bride, the Church. The wife, on her side, will seek to respond to her husband as the Church responds to Christ, the Bridegroom. Certainly, there will be faults and failings on both sides. But these will be covered over as each repents and seeks forgiveness from the other."* [10]

What, therefore, are some of the outcomes of the fear of the Lord in marriage?

Foundational understanding

Marriage is holy. It is a covenant (Malachi 2:14). It has been set apart by God for His holy purposes. It should be treated as holy and therefore we should have reverence towards it and a desire for it to remain as God intended it to be, not what mankind wants it to be. Hebrews 13:4 states, *"Marriage should be honoured by all and the marriage bed kept undefiled, for God will judge the sexually immoral and adulterers."* Marriage should be honoured and respected, not treated impartially. The fear of the Lord will strengthen our desires to honour and respect marriage and see it as a holy thing that belongs to God, not mankind.

Therefore, the fear of the Lord helps us from thinking that marriage is about us, or our spouse, or our children – but rather, it is for the Lord. It is the Lord who rules over the marriage, and we should seek to obey His instructions regarding marriage. Submitting our marriage to the Lord Jesus requires us to obey His word and seek insight and understanding. The fear of the Lord moves us to want to obey Him in marital areas.

---

[10] *'Husbands and Fathers'*, by Derek Prince, Sovereign World, pages 46/47

Invokes the spirit of submission, humility and love

Ephesians 5 is a well-known passage on Biblical marriage. It explains some of the spiritual principles behind God's design for marriage.

In short, the wife is commanded to submit to her husband as she does to the Lord (22,24,33). Why? *"For the husband is the head of the wife as Christ is the head of the church"* (v.23). Does this mean that the wife is not equal to the husband? No. We all share in the glory as heirs of God (1 Peter 3:7). The role of wives submitting to their husband is God's design and demonstration of the heavenly reality of the Church submitting to the Lord Jesus. It can be hard for the wife to find a godly motivation to submit to her husband, but the key to doing this in a godly manner is the fear of the Lord. The verse before instructing the wife to submit to her husband instructs us to submit to one another in the fear of Christ (Ephesians 5:21, NASB). It is out of fear and reverence for Christ in which wives will find the godly motivation to submit to their husbands. The wife's motivation shouldn't be for their husband's sake, but for Christ's sake. A reverence for what marriage is in the eyes of the Lord will help protect and guard marriages to be holy unto the Lord, not like the world.

My wife, Sarah, has written a testimony of how the fear of the Lord has helped her to submit to me in our marriage:

"Conversations around working out our roles as husband and wife came up early in our relationship – I see now because the Lord had a lot of undoing and teaching to do in me regarding submission! It didn't appear totally natural for me to submit deeply to Tristan as I was studying at a higher level than him when we met, I was the breadwinner when we first got married and I had strong ideas about my independence. Yet at the same time, the Holy Spirit was fast-tracking our hearts and minds as He was bringing profound understanding of the freedom of selfless love, submission to one another and the fear of the

Lord. Even in the early days of dating we were so aware of holiness that we didn't want anything to defile our relationship, which we immediately knew was destined for marriage. Unlike previous relationships, examples I had seen around me or what the world taught, I began to taste of the beauty, freedom and safety of submitting to Tristan, letting Him lead and trusting the Lord at work in him.

An early example of where I began to live with more of the fear of the Lord in our marriage, is when we moved to rent our second home, three months into our marriage. I had recently graduated and while Tristan continued to study, I was the breadwinner and so the estate agents naturally took my name and signature as the 'head tenant' for our new rental. It wasn't until we got home and checked over the documents that this phrase didn't sit at all comfortably – for Tristan! Personally, I could see the logic with my name being the one accountable for any mishaps because I was the earner, and anyway, it was just a title and really both our names were on the contract. Tristan couldn't go along with this though and explained that what is bound on earth is bound in heaven so actually the language DID matter and the overall responsibility (headship) lies with him.

I realised I had a choice whether to yield to this strange sort of thinking or fight for my right, and I concluded that Tristan's conviction was in line with Scripture (even though I didn't really understand it) so I chose to submit. He handled the situation with gentleness, respect and love, which made it easier for me to submit to his desires. He did not exalt himself over me, forcing me to obey his decision and 'put me in my place', but rather I felt totally equal and that I had the CHOICE to submit to his headship, which felt pleasing to God and Tristan.

This marked the beginning of the journey acknowledging that as my husband, Tristan is my head, and that the spiritual reality of that is undeniable. The point is that we have a choice whether or not to agree with that, and I chose on *that day to agree that Tristan is my head and has the higher spiritual responsibility in the home.*

Now, we are probably the only people to have called this estate agents to ask for our names to be switched around on a piece of paper, willingly pay £120 for them to do so (which we barely had) and drive across town to resign the contract, which in their eyes was no different. But we felt the conviction under the fear of the Lord and did it in unity. Something shifted for us as we made the "public declaration" that Tristan was in the position of headship in our marriage. It may not have changed anything in the physical realm, but spiritually we bonded as I made a choice to submit to Tristan and this has set a pathway for our marriage."

It is noted in Proverbs 31:28-31, that for wives to fear the Lord is one of the most noble and praiseworthy things they can do: *"Her children arise and call her blessed; her husband also, and he praises her: "Many women do noble things, but you surpass them all." Charm is deceptive, and beauty is fleeting;* **but a woman who fears the Lord is to be praised.** *Honour her for all that her hands have done, and let her works bring her praise at the city gate."*

I will also add that we both recognise and submit to Christ's headship, which is over all. Ultimately, we both submit to Christ and we are equal, but in the family we have our roles, just as a Pastor has a role over the deacons and congregation in a church. When it comes to making decisions, it is by God's grace that we have always been in unity for the big decisions we have made for our family, and I believe a lot of that is because we both seek the fear of the Lord and submission to Him and His word. But there is something I believe to be important, and incredibly powerful and glorifying to Christ, when a godly wife confesses that her husband is her head. Spoken 'out loud' confession is powerful! In Romans 10:9-10, we are told that, "If you declare with your mouth, "Jesus is Lord"…you will be saved…and it is with your mouth that you profess your faith and are saved." It may be easy for

Christian wives to confess, "Jesus is Lord", but I wonder how many Christian wives would willingly confess to their husband, "You are my head". I expect that simple confession may open the path of healing and restoration in many Christian marriages.

How about the husbands then? They are given their command to **love** their wives (Ephesians 5:25-28, 33). The love expressed for the wife is a love that prefers the wife, loves to serve her needs, cares for her, is patient and gentle with her, is humble, and desires for her to be holy, clean and blameless.

As a husband I see that my love for my wife is most powerfully expressed in times where I have the revelation that she belongs to the Lord and that she is His eternal bride, and I am only her earthly husband. More than anything I want to see my wife be presented holy and blameless before her heavenly husband, having flourished in life by producing the godly acts a women of the Lord should endeavour to do. I long to hear the Lord say to her, "Well done, good and faithful servant." And then when it's my turn, I long to hear Him say the same thing and be pleased with how I helped her grow in her faith in Christ. Inevitably, I will be judged by Christ for how I cared for and loved my wife, and this holy fear moves me to want to love her, serve her, be faithful to her, and build her up!

The most important relationship a husband has after the Lord, is with His wife! We must put the time, effort, prayer and love into this relationship that Christ would be expecting us to, for these women are **incredibly valuable** to Him!

Protects us from marital unfaithfulness and divorce

The divorce rate in western Christian marriages is almost the same level as it is with the world. Words fail to express the grieving of the Holy Spirit that this causes. I believe this is largely due to the lack of the fear of the Lord in Christians and their marriages. Derek Prince[11] writes *"Without the fear of the Lord, Christian marriage is on the same level as one between unbelievers. It can never become what God intends. It will lack that special flavour that should distinguish it from marriages between unbelievers."*

Though Jesus did say that marital unfaithfulness was the one reason to perhaps why a person could divorce another, I would ask the question, "Why would there be marital unfaithfulness in the first place?" The answer is a lack of the fear of the Lord. The fear of the Lord is a hatred of evil, and God hates marital unfaithfulness, and He hates divorce (Malachi 2:16) As we read earlier from Hebrews 13:4, *"the marriage bed must be kept undefiled, for God will judge the sexually immoral and adulterers."* We gain a fear of God when we realise that God hates marital unfaithfulness and will judge those who are sexually immoral or adulterers, and therefore the fear of His judgement helps us to keep away from such sins.

Jesus warns His disciples sternly, *"You have heard that it was said, 'You shall not commit adultery.' But I tell you that anyone who looks at a woman lustfully has already committed adultery with her in his heart. If your right eye causes you to stumble, gouge it out and throw it away. It is better for you to lose one part of your body than for your whole body to be thrown into hell."* (Matthew 5:27-29)

The fear of God's judgement to the adulterer will protect us from even looking at somebody lustfully. This is a dear warning to those who are stuck in the trap of pornography, particularly if you are married. It is indeed a form of adultery. I urge you with much pleading to make every effort to turn from this sin, lest be in danger of being "thrown into hell", (v.29). 1 Corinthians 6:9-11 warns us also, that no sexually immoral person will inherit the Kingdom of God.

---

[11] *'Husbands and Fathers'*, by Derek Prince, Sovereign World, page 42

We've got to take God's word seriously and should desire to be a people who *tremble at His word*. We are to study the Scriptures to know what is pleasing and not pleasing to Him, and be aware of what leads us to life, or death.

Resolving conflict in marriage

Practice the fear of the Lord in your marital conflicts by, HOLDING BACK YOUR TONGUE!

DON'T start conflict! Proverbs 17:14 says, "Starting a quarrel is like breaching a dam; so drop the matter before a dispute breaks out."

DON'T let pride (a need to be proven right), or revenge, be spoken! Proverbs 17:9 says, "Whoever conceals an offense promotes love, but he who brings it up separates friends."

DON'T speak evil, unhelpful or unwise things! Proverbs 21:23 says, "Whoever keeps his mouth and his tongue keeps himself out of trouble."

Our enemy, the devil, prowls around like a lion, waiting to find someone to devour, (1 Peter 5:8). He knows our weaknesses, and he knows how to bring division and destruction. That is what he does; that is what he longs for. Jesus tells us that Satan has come to steal, kill and destroy, (John 10:10). I believe that one of his primary focuses of attack is Christian marriages because if he is successful in that, then the children will be affected too. If the family, then, is oppressed by the devil, then that affects their fellowship with the entire Christian body. This is particularly important for those in leadership (1 Timothy 3:4-5 & 12).

Conflicting issues **will** arise in marriage, but the issue is how you deal with them. Deal with them in the fear of the Lord and in love.

Unresolved conflict in the marriage will provide a door for the enemy to work his way deeper into the marriage and family and desire to bring defilement through many different types of sin; bitterness, anger, lust, sexual immorality, unforgiveness, control and pride are some of the main sins of defilement the devil will want to destroy marriages with.

In the fear of God, we can remind ourselves of God's hatred of sin and His *delight* for those who seek to obey His commands. Be humble, honest, repentant and forgiving; preferring the other above yourself. A helpful equation to remember in times of conflict is:

Repentance + Forgiveness = Reconciliation

Chapter 18
The Fear Of The Lord In Family

There is a strong theme in Biblical literature of instructing your families in the fear of the Lord; often accompanied with wonderful blessings for those who do indeed fear Him. The Lord's desires for family are clear; His ways, His commands and His blessings are to be taught and passed on from generation to generation with fruitful multiplication.

One of the most important desires to be passed on and taught in the family line is to *fear the Lord your God*. Deuteronomy 4:10 says, *"Never forget the day when you stood before the Lord your God at Mount Sinai, where he told me, 'Summon the people before me, and I will personally instruct them. Then they will learn to fear me as long as they live, and they will teach their children to fear me also."* Something to note here is that the Lord personally instructed the people of Israel, and by doing so they learnt to fear Him as they heard directly from the Lord. But the Lord's desire was that they (the parents) would teach their children to fear Him also. This instruction to teach one's children to fear God is also beautifully spoken in Psalm 34:11, *"Come, my children, listen to me; and I will teach you the fear of the Lord"*. In this scripture there is so much hope, hope for the younger generation to sit down and hear the wisdom of God through parents. If we consider how rich the fear of the Lord is, (the beginning of wisdom, the beginning of knowledge, the treasure and delight of the Lord), it is not surprising that there is such a clear, strong and hopeful message for the parents to pass it on and teach it to their children.

The fear of the Lord is, therefore, not something that only the mature in Christ should have, but it is to be a bedrock for the young. The Lord does not want the children to be left out of growing in the fear of the Lord. Deuteronomy 31:12-13, *"Call them all together—men, women, children, and the foreigners living in your towns—so they may hear this Book of Instruction and learn to fear the Lord your God and carefully obey all the terms of these instructions. Do this **so that your children** who have not known these instructions will hear them and will learn to fear the Lord your God. Do this as long as you live in the land you are crossing the Jordan to occupy."*

All believers should be taught the fear of the Lord but in these scriptures, there is an emphasis on teaching it to the children because that is the way God intends it to carry on down the generations. Christian parents have an enormous responsibility to teach their children the fear of the Lord. We must not put this aside. In a current generation where some of the Church in the West is turning away from the true and most holy faith towards beliefs and practices that are an abomination to the Lord, one can only wonder if that is a direct result of the 1960's "Aquarius" generation that somewhat rebelled against the fear of the Lord, and thus withheld from teaching their children to truly fear God. As parents teach their children to fear the Lord, they will no doubt grow in respect in the eyes of their children also. A respect and submission to elders is a holy thing for children to grow up in, and as we near the return of Christ, this will be something forcefully targeted by the enemy. As we are warned in 2 Timothy 3:1-2, *"But mark this: There will be terrible times in the last days. People will be lovers of themselves, lovers of money, boastful, proud, abusive, **disobedient to their parents**, ungrateful, unholy."* And in 2 Peter 2:10, *"He [God] is especially hard on those who follow their own twisted sexual desire, and **who despise authority**.*

These people are proud and arrogant, daring even to scoff at supernatural beings without so much as trembling."

Parents should teach and instruct their children in the fear of the Lord in light of end times and the coming judgements of God. A wonderful example of this is by the actions and motives of the great man of faith, Noah:

"By faith Noah, when warned about things not yet seen, in holy fear built an ark to save his family." (Hebrews 11:7a)

So much can be grasped from this one verse, but again we see that when a man or woman of God is given prophetic insight into the coming judgements and wrath of God, they are moved in a fear of God to do what God commands us, to protect their family from that coming judgement.

But what does this look like practically? Below are some thoughts to consider:

1) **The parents themselves are to grow in the fear of the Lord.** If the parents themselves don't fear God, they will not be able to teach or instruct their children in it. Children will be convicted of the importance and outworking of the fear of the Lord when they see it authentically demonstrated to them by their parents. I encourage every parent to make extra effort towards growing in the fear of the Lord, and I hope this book contributes to the growth of it in your life. The final chapter of this book gives some helpful practical advice on how to grow in the fear of the Lord.

2) **Parents are to "teach" their children the fear of the Lord.** As I mentioned above, the most impactful element of teaching the fear of the Lord to your children is by demonstrating it yourselves.

But there is also a need for verbal teaching and instruction. Psalm 34:11 paints this picture well. "Come my children and listen to me, and I will teach you the fear of the Lord." It is an incredibly valuable part of Christian family life to sit down together and read the Bible, read a devotion, pray, or discuss spiritual matters. It is often in these environments that we can teach them the fear of the Lord. These can be godly rhythms you have in place as a family, but of course some of the most impactful moments of sitting down with a child and teaching them the wisdom of the Lord is when something out of the ordinary happens and the Lord leads you to a unique time to sit down with them and teach them or comfort them with wisdom from God. A large proportion of teaching children about the fear of the Lord is teaching them that there are consequences to their actions and the decisions that they make. There must also be forgiveness and mercy.

3) **Parents are to pray regularly that their children will learn to fear God.** It is God's desire that your children will grow in the fear of the Lord, and when we pray anything in line with His will, we know that he hears it and answers (1 John 5:14-15). Another thing to consider is what the Apostle Paul spoke of in 1 Corinthians 3. He shared the spiritual principle that one person may sow a seed (of the word), another may water that seed, but only God can make it grow (1 Corinthians 3:7), and what's important is that God is the One who makes it grow. We must sow seeds by speaking and demonstrating the fear of the Lord for our children. We must water these seeds through prayer and repeated demonstration and teaching, but only God can cause the fear of the Lord to grow in their lives! So pray that He will!

4) **Do not forsake disciplining your children.** Let us consider the following scriptures:

> **1 Samuel 3:11-13,** *"Then the Lord said to Samuel, 'I am about to do a shocking thing in Israel. I am going to carry out all my threats against Eli and his family, from beginning to end. I have warned him that judgment is coming upon his family forever, because his sons are blaspheming God and he hasn't disciplined them.'"*
>
> **1 Samuel 2:29-30** *"So why do you scorn my sacrifices and offerings? Why do you give your sons more honour than you give me—for you and they have become fat from the best offerings of my people Israel! 'Therefore, the Lord, the God of Israel, says: I promised that your branch of the tribe of Levi would always be my priests. But I will honour those who honour me, and I will despise those who think lightly of me.'"*
>
> **Proverbs 13:24,** *"Whoever spares the rod hates his son, but he who loves him is diligent to discipline him."*
>
> **Proverbs 23:13-14,** *"Do not withhold discipline from a child; if you strike him with a rod, he will not die. If you strike him with the rod, you will save his soul from Sheol."*

Scripture is clear that it is right and God-intended for parents to discipline their children. There is wisdom needed for what that looks like of course, and we are reminded in Ephesians 6:4, *"Fathers, do not provoke your children to anger, but bring them up in the discipline and instruction of the Lord."* Indeed, the fear of the Lord should encourage parents to discipline their children, but also protect parents from disciplining wrongly and harshly, *"Show your fear of God by not treating them harshly"*. (Leviticus 25:43)

5) **Be aware of the devil's tactics and overcome these things with the truth, even perhaps before they are seen.** Be warned of the dangers of the last days. 2 Timothy 3:1-5, Paul writes to Timothy;

"You should know this, Timothy, that in the last days there will be very difficult times. For people will love only themselves and their money. They will be boastful and proud, scoffing at God, disobedient to their parents, and ungrateful. They will consider nothing sacred. They will be unloving and unforgiving; they will slander others and have no self-control. They will be cruel and hate what is good. They will betray their friends, be reckless, be puffed up with pride, and love pleasure rather than God. They will act religious, but they will reject the power that could make them godly. Stay away from people like that!"

When we read through this list of sins that will be prevalent in the last days, we can see how much a blessing it will be for those who fear the Lord as this will indeed protect them from such sins.

It is well known as the fourth commandment of the law given to Moses, that children must *"Honour your father and mother, so that your days may be long in the land that the LORD your God is giving you"* (Exodus 20:12). This is recited by Jesus (Matthew 15:4-6) and also the New Testament Apostles (Ephesians 6:1-3). It is, therefore, important to teach and train our children to obey this valuable command but not in a dominating, controlling, intimidating or manipulative way, but in the Spirit of the fear of the Lord.

Ephesians 6:4 expresses a direct command to fathers (not forsaking mothers) on the way they act with their children. *"Fathers, do not provoke your children to anger, but bring them up in the discipline and instruction of the Lord."* The NIV says, "Fathers, do not exasperate your children", but the majority of translations expresses in more simple terms what the command is. It is helpful to read the amplified translation regarding this phrase. *"Fathers, do not provoke your children to anger [do not exasperate them to the point of resentment with demands that are trivial or unreasonable or humiliating or abusive; nor by showing favouritism or indifference to any of them]."*

I find it interesting that there is just one command given here to parents! I would have liked several so that I could have more insight into raising godly children. But I believe there is only one here because the Apostle Paul, under the wisdom of the Holy Spirit, knew the sin that most commonly affected the fathers in their parenting. And that is that in their desire for high standards for their children, and perhaps a lack of sympathy to their childlikeness, they would act in a way that inevitably provoked their children to anger.

The instruction to parents goes on to say, *"but bring them up in the discipline and instruction of the Lord"*. The Greek words "paideia", meaning discipline, and "nouthesia", meaning instruction (or more precisely, admonition), are defined as, "the rearing of a child, training, discipline, education of children, instruction, chastisement, correction, warning, admonition, and counsel." Parents are to administer these things to their children, but that can be done in God's way, or not God's way, and the fear of the Lord will help you administer these in God's way.

Continuing the theme of anger, I think most parents amongst us can confess that parenting can at times be very frustrating, and when our "buttons can get pushed" and our patience is tested then we can often slip into anger. There has been a time in my parenting thus far where I have fallen into too many angry outbursts. The following words of Jesus gripped me with the fear of God, and with deep conviction I repented and there was significant breakthrough in that area, (though I continue to work out my salvation in fear and trembling). Jesus speaks in Matthew 5:21-24, *"You have heard that our ancestors were told, 'You must not murder. If you commit murder, you are subject to judgment.' But I say, if you are even angry with someone, you are subject to judgment! If you call someone an idiot, you are in danger of being brought before the court. And if you curse someone, you are in danger of the fires of hell."*

James 1:19-20 says, *"My dear brothers and sisters, take note of this: Everyone should be quick to listen, slow to speak and slow to become angry, because human anger does not produce the righteousness that God desires."* Human anger, which is sin, does not produce the righteousness of God, but produces footholds that our enemy, the Devil, can hold on us. *"In your anger do not sin, do not give the devil a foothold."* (Ephesians 4:26). These scriptures struck me and gave me more of the fear of the Lord, and in the grace of God I was able to overcome much more of my angry desires and continued to resist them. When you continue to resist the devil and break ungodly cycles by producing godly cycles, there is deliverance. (James 4:7)

I am in awe at the blessings the Lord wants to give families and our children. Here are some incredible promises, but they are *conditional;* the condition is to *fear God!*

Psalm 103:17 *"But from everlasting to everlasting the Lord's love is with those who fear him, and his righteousness with their children's children."*

Psalm 112:1-3 *"Praise the Lord! How joyful are those who fear the Lord and delight in obeying his commands. Their children will be successful everywhere; an entire generation of godly people will be blessed. They themselves will be wealthy, and their good deeds will last forever."*

Psalm 115:13 *"He will bless those who fear the Lord, both great and lowly."*

Psalm 128:1-4 *"Blessed are all who fear the Lord, who walk in obedience to him. You will eat the fruit of your labour; blessings and prosperity will be yours. Your wife will be like a fruitful vine within your house; your children will be* *like olive shoots around your table. Yes, this will be the blessing for the man who fears the Lord."*

Proverbs 31:28-30 *"Her children arise and call her blessed; her husband also, and he praises her: "Many women do noble things, but you surpass them all." Charm is deceptive, and beauty is fleeting; but a woman who fears the Lord is to be praised."*

Chapter 19
The Fear Of The Lord In The Workplace

The workplace is most commonly a place of hierarchal structure, where people are employed in a certain role and work under people and have people under them. Many have an element of responsibility, and many will have personal struggles within the workplace. But the question is, how do we approach and deal with these issues?

The importance of submitting to authority

In Genesis 16, when Abraham slept with Hagar to conceive a child, at first Hagar began to despise her mistress, Sarai (v.4). Afterwards, Sarai then began to mistreat Hagar (v.6) and so Hagar then fled from her workplace. After fleeing from the workplace, the Angel of the Lord came to her and spoke these words:

"Hagar, slave of Sarai, where have you come from, and where are you going?"

"I'm running away from my mistress Sarai," she answered.

*Then the angel of the Lord told her, "Go back to your mistress **and submit to her**."* (Genesis 16:8-9)

Even though there had been rivalry between both Hagar and Sarai, and both had acted wrongly, the servant was told to return to her place of work and submit to authority. Why? Because the Lord knows *this is the right thing to do!*

Romans 13:1-5 is a very direct word from Apostle Paul on our attitude towards secular governing bodies. If you are in a secular workplace, we need to recognise that all authority is given by God, and we must respect what God has put in place. The leader themselves may be an unjust, ungodly person who doesn't fear God, but we do not repay evil for evil. The fear of the Lord will keep us from doing things such as gossip, rebellion and having bitter root judgements. Quite the opposite, Jesus tells us to pray for those who persecute us, to repay evil with good, and to love; for in doing so, you "pour burning coals on their head" (Proverbs 25:21-22).

Furthermore, Ephesians 6:5-8 says, *"Slaves, obey your earthly masters with respect and fear, and with sincerity of heart, just as you would obey Christ. Obey them not only to win their favour when their eye is on you, but as slaves of Christ, doing the will of God from your heart. Serve wholeheartedly, as if you were serving the Lord, not people, because you know that the Lord will reward each one for whatever good they do, whether they are slave or free."*

A further element of submitting to authority is also the time to discern when it is right to **NOT** submit to authority. This should not be considered lightly, or with any essence of rebellion. Rather, it is to be done in a God-fearing attitude, aware that you'll have to one day stand in the presence of Christ's judgements for your actions, and He will know every hidden motive of your heart!

There are some Biblical examples of when the righteous chose to disobey higher authority, and the fear of the Lord and desire to obey God, was their just reason to disobey.

Exodus 1:15-17, *"Then Pharaoh, the king of Egypt, gave this order to the Hebrew midwives, Shiphrah and Puah: 'When you help the Hebrew women as they give birth, watch as they deliver. If the baby is a boy, kill him; if it is a girl, let her live.'* ***But because the midwives feared God, they refused to obey the king's orders.*** *They allowed the boys to live, too."*

Acts 4:18-20, *"Then they called them in again and commanded them not to speak or teach at all in the name of Jesus. But Peter and John replied, 'Which is right in God's eyes: to listen to you, or to him? You be the judges! As for us, we cannot help speaking about what we have seen and heard.'"*

The importance of the fear of the Lord in leadership

The other element of working in the workplace is that you may be in a position of leadership. You may not be the CEO, but you may have a small team who you lead. As in Ephesians 6:7-8, leaders also must 'serve wholeheartedly' for we know that "the Lord will reward each one for whatever good they do".

Ephesians 6:9 goes on to say, *"And masters, treat your slaves in the same way. Do not threaten them, since you know that he who is both their Master and yours is in heaven, and there is no favouritism with him."*

The fear of the Lord and awareness of His judgement of all our works, both good and bad, will help us to, *"Care for the flock that God has entrusted to you. Watch over it willingly, not grudgingly—not for what you will get out of it, but because you are eager to serve God. Don't lord it over the people assigned to your care, but lead them by your own good example."* (1 Peter 5:2-3)

In essence, the leader is to seek humility and a servant style of leadership. This is the Lord's way, *"let the greatest among you become as the youngest, and the leader as one who serves."* (Luke 22:26, ESV)

Chapter 20
The Fear Of The Lord In Intercession

There are many kinds of prayers (1 Timothy 2:1, Ephesians 6:18) and intercession is one of those kinds. Intercession is a form of prayer which is particularly intimate with the Lord as one of its foundational expressions, "paga", literally means 'to meet with'. The term 'intercession' holds more weight when we see that it means to 'stand in the gap' between two parties; namely God and then someone or people group on the earth.

This position and calling to intercede requires the intercessor to intimately know the character and nature of God, to then 'meet with' God, whilst 'standing in the gap' and then *mediate* between Him and another person or people group. This is particularly relevant when we understand that the main biblical purpose of intercession is to stand in the gap between God and those who are deserving His angry judgement. Therefore, it is necessary for the intercessor to have a healthy and right fear of God, knowing He is holy and just to pour out His wrath and punishment.

Derek Prince writes: *The intercessor is one who comes in between. In between who? The answer is in between God and those who deserve the just wrath and punishment of God. The intercessor is one who steps in between. He lifts up his hands to Almighty God and he says, "God, these people deserve your judgment. You have every right to smite them. But if you smite them, you'll have to smite me first because I'm standing in between you and them."* [12]

One of the clearest explanations of intercession in Scripture, I believe, is in Ezekiel 22:30-31. God had been speaking against Jerusalem for all its sins, proclaiming His judgement. The Lord God finishes by saying, *"I looked for someone among them who would build up the wall and* **stand before me in the gap on behalf of the land** *so I would not have to destroy it, but I found no one. So I will pour out my wrath on them and consume them with my fiery anger, bringing down on their own heads all they have done, declares the Sovereign Lord."*

We can determine, therefore, some of the key requirements of intercession. In order to stand in the gap between God and those deserving His punishment, the intercessor must be aware of:

1: God's anger and hatred of sin, and the reality of His just judgements. This is where we 'meet with' God, knowing His heart, character and nature and can confess the sins of the people, understanding that the sins are an abomination to God because He is holy.

2: The intercessor must know the fullness of God's character by knowing His desire for mercy and to relent from His anger, which is why the intercessor can plead for mercy.

3: The intercessor must be repentant themselves, seeking to walk in holiness. God would not listen to a person who was asking God for mercy for a sin someone else were committing if they themselves were

---

[12] https://www.derekprince.com/sermons/227

unaware and unrepentant of the plank in their own eye. Hence the prayers of the righteous are powerful and effective! (James 5:16).

4: The intercessor should be willing to lay down their life for the sake of others.

Let us look at a few Biblical Intercessors:

Jesus Christ: The Lamb of God, sent to stand in the gap between God and the world. Jesus fully knew the righteous judgements of God that all humanity deserves. He was sent to be the perfect, total intercessor, taking the wrath and anger of God upon Himself, that God may relent of His wrath towards the world through repentance and faith in Jesus. Isaiah prophesied *"It was the Lord's will to crush Him."* (Isaiah 53:10). Jesus continues to stand in the gap between us and God, interceding between the two parties with the eternal shedding of His blood (Romans 8:34).

Abraham: Abraham's encounter with the Lord in Genesis 18:16-33, looking out over Sodom and Gomorrah, is a foundational framework for intercession. In verse 17 the Lord says, "Shall I hide from Abraham what I am about to do?" This speaks of the relationship already forged between Abraham and God. God has seen his faith and counts him as righteous. God has seen Abraham's obedience which is a true mark of fearing God. And in this Scripture, we learn that God chooses whom to share His inner most thoughts and plans of judgement and wrath with, and Abraham has proved himself one whom the Lord confides in. *"The Lord confides in those who fear him".* (Psalm 25:14a)

The Lord shared His plans of judgement to Abraham because He knew Abraham's heart and would be pleased to receive His pleads of mercy for the righteous. As a result of Abraham's intercessions, God changed

His plans and relented from pouring out His wrath on Sodom and Gomorrah until the righteous had escaped.

Moses: Moses was one who had such a close friendship with God that it is written *"God spoke to Moses, face to face, as one speaks to a friend."* (Exodus 33:11). How wonderful, again, that we are seeing and desiring intimate friendship with God. When we look through conversations between God and Moses more thoroughly though, we see how their friendship involves God sharing His Heart with Moses, often expressing His emotions such as anger and disappointment. I believe this shows the depth of friendship God had with Moses, that He was willing to share such deep and personal things.

God speaks with intercessors, with those who fear God about His more inner thoughts. He shares His secrets with those who fear Him because they can relate somewhat to what He feels in His hatred and disappointment at sin, and because they can relate to Him, they also respond in a way that is pleasing to Him. This is what we see with Moses.

When Israel sinned against the Lord, provoking His anger by building a calf and worshipping it as the Lord, (Exodus 32:7-14) God shared His plans with Moses, concluding in verse 10 *"Now leave me alone so that my anger may burn against them and that I may destroy them. Then I will make you into a great nation."* But Moses acted as an intercessor and spoke with the Lord, and the Lord relented from His wrath.

The Lord again expresses His anger and plans for punishment against Israel in Numbers 14:11-25. "Then the Lord said to Moses: *'How long will these people reject Me? And how long will they not believe Me, with all the signs which I have performed among them? I will strike them with the pestilence and disinherit them, and I will make of you a nation greater and mightier than they.'"* (Vs 11-12). Moses then interceded and God relented.

Apostle Paul: The Apostle Paul interceded for the people of Israel in a Christ-like way; being willing to eternally perish for the salvation of Israel. Romans 9:1-3 says, *"With Christ as my witness, I speak with utter truthfulness. My conscience and the Holy Spirit confirm it. My heart is filled with bitter sorrow and unending grief for my people, my Jewish brothers and sisters. I would be willing to be forever cursed—cut off from Christ!—if that would save them."*

In all these examples, the intercessor was aware of God's anger, just judgements, the coming wrath, eternal damnation, and thus they could intercede. These harder parts of God's heart and nature are not to be ignored but fully understood. It is God's good invitation to invite His people to that secret place of His inner most thoughts so that we may cry out for mercy.

In the beginning of this book, we spoke about how the fear of the Lord comes at the revelation that the Holy God **hates** sin, and He gives this same hatred of sin to those who fear Him. I remember a time when I approached the Lord in prayer and asked Him, *"Lord, what do you hate?"* I was excited and hopeful at the prospect of being welcomed into a deeper friendship with God, yet at the same time humbled and in holy fear of His awesomeness and holiness.

The answer came immediately as I became aware of the covenant unfaithfulness of Israel; how they continued to receive God's mercy, yet still rebelled again and again by prostituting themselves to idols. I began to feel very heavy with the weight of how created sinful people could constantly commit spiritual adultery with such an incredibly gracious, committed and faithful Creator God. As I was heavy in my spirit with this burden, the Lord then spoke directly to my spirit, "I hate divorce" (Malachi 2:16). I curled over in grief and agony with a deeper reality of how dreadful we, the Church, have been regarding divorce. With divorce rates in the western church almost as high as the sinful world, in the sight of the Holy covenant making God, I was - for a minute or two - deeply overwhelmed with our sin. I could barely speak, but repeatedly cried out, "Lord have mercy, we have sinned". After a few minutes of travailing, I calmed in intercession – perhaps the Lord had heard my prayer.

The story goes on that 5 weeks later I heard something extraordinary from two of my friends who were both Christian male ministers. They told me that 5 weeks earlier (at the time of my intercession) their hidden sin of watching pornography was **exposed!** Both were unknown of each other's circumstances or my intercessions, and both of them were in marriage relationships.

When deep, hidden sins are exposed, it doesn't feel pleasant at the time, but it is far more important to bring to light what is hidden, rather than allowing sin to defile the body and spirit of the believer (2 Corinthians 7:1). Hebrews 12:10-11 says, *"Our fathers disciplined us for a short time as they thought best, but God disciplines us for our good, so that we may share in His holiness. No discipline seems enjoyable at the time, but painful. Later on, however, it yields a harvest of righteousness and peace to those who have been trained by it."*

I believe that as I partnered with God's hatred of sin (divorce and covenant unfaithfulness/adultery), and interceded for mercy, God in His kindness broke through into at least two Christian minister's lives to expose a deep sin that was surely going to cause more harm if ignored. The couples could then start a healing journey, with God's grace and with the support of the Body, and can walk towards healing, restoration and more holiness in their marriage.

Confessing (in intercessory prayer) the sins of others in the fear of the Lord, moves God's mercy to bring about greater holiness in His Church!

On a side note; intercession is a MUCH bigger topic than what I have covered, but for the purpose of this book I wanted to give some insight into how the fear of the Lord operates in intercession.

Intercession for healing the land

Another component of intercession is in the priestly role of interceding on behalf of the sins on the land (2 Chronicles 7:14, Leviticus 26:40-42). Scripture is clear, that sin defiles the land and can even bring a curse on the land. Five sins, in particular, bring defilement and curse on the land:

1: Idolatry (Jeremiah 3:6-10)
2: Broken covenants (2 Samuel 21:1)
3: Sexual sin (Leviticus 18:24-25). Context Leviticus 18:6-23
4: Bloodshed (Numbers 35:33-34)
5: Broken families (Malachi 4:6)

Let us consider a real-life situation in England. In June, 2024, 700 people gathered in Trafalgar Square, London, to perform Hindu worship, called, 'yoga'. Unfortunately, there is deception in the Church and a lack of the fear of God that brings many Christians to think that performing yoga is not a sin and that it is not idolatry! Some Christians even do it in the name of Christ!! It is often allowed in our places of worship, which will bring defilement in that place. How has the Church got to this state? Because it lacks the fear of God! In Jeremiah 3:8-9, God says *"I gave faithless Israel her certificate of divorce and sent her away because of all her adulteries. Yet I saw that her unfaithful sister Judah **had no fear; she also went out and committed adultery.** Because Israel's immorality mattered so little to her, **she defiled the land** and committed adultery with stone and wood."*

What do people think when we speak of these things? If we are unaware or do not believe that God brings judgement to idolatry and worship of demons, then there is no need to confess sin. But there are curses and defilement on the land and God HATES these sins of idolatry. Those who fear the Lord can then grieve with Him about these sins and cry out for mercy. The one who does not hate this sin and know in their spirit how much God hates it cannot effectively partner with God in intercession to heal the land.

For more insight on healing the land I suggest reading "God's Footprint on the Land", by Dr. Alistair Petrie.

Chapter 21
The Fear Of The Lord In The Unifying Of Believers

For the Body of Christ to live and work well amongst each other we must have the fear of the Lord. In the heart of humanity are such things as greed, envy, jealousy, selfish ambition, and pride. These at work amongst the believers are the cause for so much of the division and unforgiveness that we experience in the Body of Christ. One powerful tool to loosen these bonds of wickedness off the Church is the simple instruction in Ephesians 5:21, *"Subject yourselves to one another in the fear of Christ."* (NASB)

If we all took this on board much of the selfish ambition and pride that causes disagreements and divisions amongst us would be broken. Where some are furious that things are not done 'their way', we should submit to one another. When some are controlling or dominating amongst other believers, we should submit to one another. The Holy Spirit works in the believers to live in this way, as it is the way of Christ.

As the above Scripture reveals, the motivation and power that God gives the Church to submit to one another is the fear of God. The revelation is not "Submit to one another out of a love for Christ". The revelation is to "Submit to one another out of fear of Christ". I have experienced myself and witnessed amongst others how difficult it can be to submit to one another. We can try to conjure up the power to do it, but without God, we can't. The power that God gives us to fulfil this command is the fear of the Lord. When you are afraid of God's judgement on those who cause ungodly divisions and fights amongst believers, you will stop doing it, out of a fear of God, and instead you would pursue acts of love for others, and God would fill your heart more and more with His love.

Why fear God's judgement regarding this? 1 Corinthians 3:16-17 states:

"Don't you know that you yourselves are God's temple and that God's Spirit dwells in your midst? If anyone destroys God's temple, God will destroy that person; for God's temple is sacred, and you together are that temple."

How can there be divisions and quarrelling amongst us when we see that each of us are God's temple and when we speak or do things against each other we are destroying God's temple! *"If anyone destroys God's temple, God will destroy that person"*. Let us rather submit to God and to one another. Let us throw off the things that entangle us and cause us to sin against each other and reverently submit to one another, for Christ will judge us all. Further guidance on this is in James 4:1-12.

What does God think about stirring up division in the Church? God not only hates it, but considers it an abomination!

There are six things that the Lord hates,
seven that are an abomination to him:
haughty eyes, a lying tongue,
and hands that shed innocent blood,
a heart that devises wicked plans,

> *feet that make haste to run to evil,*
> *a false witness who breathes out lies,*
> *and one who sows discord among brothers.*

(Proverbs 6:16-19)

God hates sowing discord among brethren with a detestable passion. I used to find myself speaking against other denominations. Though I wasn't fervent in this, I still knew my heart and subtly let out complaints and undermining comments. It was when I read Proverbs 6 that the fear of the Lord struck me so powerfully, I deeply repented and now live in a state where I am much more cautious of what I say. Is my heart perfect? No, I don't believe it is yet, but the fear of God brought me to a deep repentance and my attitude towards the worldwide Church and its different denominations and practices has transformed hugely and I now have a love, thankfulness, and respect for others that I did not have before. Now, if any tempting thought comes my way that makes me want to say something ungodly about a fellow believer or the Church, the fear of God in me strengthens me to resist that sin and I have now found a new strength in me to value others above myself.

Using this testimony as an example, if we continue to sin in one area the devil can gain a foothold, or even stronghold on that area (Ephesians 4:26). For example, if someone spoke against the Body of believers and did not repent, ungodly footholds such as a root of bitterness or a judgemental/critical spirit could come in and take root. However, if, in the fear of God, someone continues to resist the temptation to speak against other believers, then the devil's hold would be loosened, and any ungodly root or spirit would lose its foothold and can be demolished. For the command is to *"Submit to God, resist the devil and he will flee from you."* (James 4:7). We need the fear of God to strengthen our capacity to resist the devil and say "no" to temptation.

The importance of forgiveness in the Body of Christ

We are commanded by the Lord and by the early Apostles to forgive each other. This is particularly relevant for the Church, to forgive the brethren, (Ephesians 4:32). This is absolutely done with a motivation of love *"because the Lord forgave you"*. But we need to wake up to the reality of God's judgement on the believer if we refuse to forgive each other. Do you know that there are consequences if we choose not to forgive? God warns us again and again that if we hold back forgiveness from a fellow believer, then there are just consequences right at our door. If you are wise, and fear God, we will do well to pay special attention to these warnings to the Church.

When Jesus was teaching His disciples how to pray, He taught them *"Forgive us our sins, as we forgive those who sin against us"* (Matthew 6:12). Jesus explains the reason behind this in verses 14-15, *"For if you forgive other people when they sin against you, your heavenly Father will also forgive you. But if you do not forgive others their sins, your Father will **not** forgive your sins."*

I fear that we in the western evangelical church have generally undermined this Scripture to align with our theology. It comes straight from the mouth of Jesus, and He doesn't delude us with twisted words – He is direct as needs be! Jesus is talking to the children of God, "Your heavenly Father" and warns them that once they receive forgiveness of their sins and fail to forgive others of their sins then they provoke the anger and judgements of God upon themselves and ***there will be torture!*** Read below the Parable of the unmerciful servant. (Matthew 18:21-35)

Then Peter came to Jesus and asked, "Lord, how many times shall I forgive my brother or sister who sins against me? Up to seven times?"

Jesus answered, "I tell you, not seven times, but seventy-seven times.

"Therefore, the kingdom of heaven is like a king who wanted to settle accounts with his servants. As he began the settlement, a man who owed him ten thousand bags of gold was brought to him. Since he was not able to pay, the master ordered that he and his wife and his children and all that he had be sold to repay the debt.

"At this the servant fell on his knees before him. 'Be patient with me,' he begged, 'and I will pay back everything.' The servant's master took pity on him, cancelled the debt and let him go.

"But when that servant went out, he found one of his fellow servants who owed him a hundred silver coins. He grabbed him and began to choke him. 'Pay back what you owe me!' he demanded.

"His fellow servant fell to his knees and begged him, 'Be patient with me, and I will pay it back.'

"But he refused. Instead, he went off and had the man thrown into prison until he could pay the debt. When the other servants saw what had happened, they were outraged and went and told their master everything that had happened.

"Then the master called the servant in. 'You wicked servant,' he said, 'I cancelled all that debt of yours because you begged me to. Shouldn't you have had mercy on your fellow servant just as I had on you?' In anger his master handed him over to the jailers to be tortured, until he should pay back all he owed.

"This is how my heavenly Father will treat each of you unless you forgive your brother or sister from your heart."

In the fear of God, if you are holding a grudge against anyone, or want revenge, repent, and forgive them. I realise that for many this can be a very hard thing to do, or we may not even know what it means to forgive.

One of the hardest realities of forgiving people who have hurt us is the pain that we feel. This isn't to be ignored. You may have been treated unjustly in many ways. You may have been hurt by the people who should have loved you the most, either family, or fellow believers. God knows the pain and Jesus feels that pain too, as when one part of the Body hurts, they all hurt, and that includes Jesus who is the head!

Forgiveness doesn't mean that the person 'gets away' with the injustice. It means that we choose not to judge the person ourselves, as we realise that Jesus will judge them.

"Do not repay anyone evil for evil. Be careful to do what is right in the eyes of everyone. If it is possible, as far as it depends on you, live at peace with everyone. Do not take revenge, my dear friends, but leave room for God's wrath, for it is written: 'It is mine to avenge; I will repay,' says the Lord. On the contrary: 'If your enemy is hungry, feed him; if he is thirsty, give him something to drink. In doing this, you will heap burning coals on his head.' Do not be overcome by evil, but overcome evil with good." (Romans 12:17-21)

Forgiveness is removing someone **off** our hook of judgement and placing them on the Lord's hook of judgement. We 'release' the person to the Lord Jesus, and He will have His say.

However, forgiveness can be a journey. It starts with our own choice to forgive, and the more we forgive and walk in forgiveness, our emotions may begin to be healed. Then as we continue to walk on the journey of forgiving, then it comes to our heart and we forgive from the heart, which is the Lord's desire.

We know when we have reached forgiveness from our heart. When we have reached a place of love for the person (who may even be our enemy), it would be our hearts desire that they would NOT receive punishment and wrath of God for what they have done, but instead we would hope that God would have mercy on them too. We would echo Christ's prayer on the cross, "Father forgive them, for they do not know what they do." (Luke 23:24)

The fear of the Lord helps with this, as when we feel some love or mercy towards a person, we would not want them to suffer the fire and angry wrath of God that those who fear Him know of! Therefore, we would hope on their behalf that God would have mercy on them, and they would repent of their sin.

Building unity amongst believers

As previously mentioned in Chapter 3, the path to Christian unity is holiness. This is understood from Jesus's prayer in John 17:11, "Holy Father, **protect them,** by the power of your name, the name you gave me, **so** *that they will be one, as you and I are one."*

Jesus prays and desires for His flock to be protected/set-apart from the evil one. The Lord wants us to walk in holiness and not be deceived into the ways of darkness. This is the key to "oneness", as the Lord asks the Father to protect His people **SO THAT** they will be one! The fear of the Lord is key to working out this holiness and unity!

Key to the strength and increase of the Church

Another aspect which I find most exhilarating is to know that the fear of the Lord is a key to the strengthening and increase of the Church. In Acts 9:31, it is recorded, *"So the church throughout all Judea and Galilee and Samaria had peace and was being built up. And walking in the fear of the*

Lord and in the comfort of the Holy Spirit, it multiplied." The NLT says, "The church then had peace throughout Judea, Galilee, and Samaria, and it became stronger as the believers lived in the fear of the Lord. And with the encouragement of the Holy Spirit, it also grew in numbers."

We take into account the context. Just four chapters earlier in the records of the early Church, it is recorded that Ananias and Sapphira died because of their sin against the Holy Spirit. What happened as a result of this? ***"And great fear came over the whole church and all who heard about these events."*** (Acts 5:11)

The Church had experienced the judgement of God, even against the believer, and the result was a holy fear. But as the Church lived in the fear of the Lord AND in the encouragement of the Holy Spirit amidst miracles and signs and wonders, **the Church was strengthened and increased in numbers!**

Simply put: Any Church leader who is hungry for an increase of numbers and a strengthening of the flock should desire to grow in the fear the Lord and seek the Spirit's encouragement through miracles and signs and wonders.

Chapter 22
The Fear Of The Lord In Evangelism

As with much of what I have talked about, the evangelist's heart will do well to have both love and fear. The issue we face is when there is one, and not the other. If people were to picture in their minds a preacher evangelising in the fear of God, they may picture someone standing on the street corner shouting "Repent or burn in hell". But as I have already voiced, the pendulum has now swung so much the other way, we seek to evangelise in love alone, without the fear of God.

How can the fear of the Lord motivate and empower our evangelism? It comes from a revelation of God's judgement on the unrepentant sinner.

The issue that hell is rarely preached from the pulpits is likely a great cause for the lack of the fear of the Lord in the Church today. Theologies such as universalism (the belief that all will eventually go to heaven) have spread across the church like wildfire recently as it can sit better with people's view of what God is like. Some believers have chosen not to believe in hell at all!

It is helpful for us to consider some Biblical truths of God's punishment on the unrepentant sinner.

- Hell is real!
- Hell has been created by God, for His purposes. (Matthew 25:41)
- Hell is a place of God's wrath for the wicked. (Revelation 21:8)
- Hell is eternal. (2 Thessalonians 1:9)
- Hell is a place of eternal punishment. (Jude 1:7)
- Hell is a place where the resurrected wicked (Spirit, Soul, Body) will remain. (Daniel 12:2)
- It is the same place that the devil and his demons will remain. (Revelation 20:10)
- It is scriptural that more people go to hell than to heaven. (Matthew 7:13-14)

Jesus spoke more about hell than anyone else recorded in Scripture. He constantly warned people of this reality as God's desire is for none to perish, but for all to come to repentance (2 Peter 3:9). This is God's desire, but it's also true that His wrath remains on the wicked (Romans 1:18-32).

The Apostle Paul clearly evangelised with the fear of the Lord too. The Gospel that he preached was largely based on the coming judgement (Romans 2:16). He warned people of the coming judgement, as Christ had demonstrated, and the Holy Spirit still confirmed. In the context of 'judgement' Paul writes in 2 Corinthians 5:11, *"Since, then, we know what it is to fear the Lord, we try to persuade others."*

Here are a few helpful commentaries[13] on this verse:

Benson commentary: *Knowing therefore the terror of the Lord — The strict judgment which must then pass on all impenitent sinners; we the more earnestly persuade men — To repent and believe the gospel, that, instead of being objects of the divine wrath, they may live and die happy in his favour.*

---

[13] https://biblehub.com/commentaries/2_corinthians/5-11.htm

Matthew Henry's concise commentary: *The apostle quickens himself and others to acts of duty. Well-grounded hopes of heaven will not encourage sloth and sinful security. Let all consider the judgment to come, which is called, The terror of the Lord. Knowing what terrible vengeance the Lord would execute upon the workers of iniquity, the apostle and his brethren used every argument and persuasion, to lead men to believe in the Lord Jesus, and to act as his disciples.*

Barnes' Notes on the Bible commentary: *It will be a day of awful wailing and alarm when all the living and the dead shall be arraigned on trial with reference to their eternal destiny; and when countless hosts of the guilty and impenitent shall be thrust down to an eternal hell. Who can describe the amazing terror of the scene? Who can fancy the horrors of the hosts of the guilty and the wretched who shall then hear that their doom is to be fixed forever in a world of unspeakable woe? The influence of the knowledge of the terror of the Lord on the mind of the apostle seems to have been two-fold; first, an apprehension of it as a personal concern, and a desire to escape it, which led him to constant self-denial and toil; and secondly, a desire to save others from being overwhelmed in the wrath of that dreadful day.*

When the preacher or evangelist knows what it means to fear the Lord, he or she knows that all will one day be judged, and therefore, tries to persuade people to turn to Christ and be saved.

A meditative look at Revelation 20:11-15 should invoke the fear of the Lord in us, for the perishing sinner. We should have a godly anxiety for the sinner, because we know something of what they are on their way to, and yet they remain oblivious or unrepentant. They are walking not just towards a cliff-face where they would tumble to their death, but are heading towards eternal punishment due to a life in rebellion to the God of the Universe. We have the answer, we know the Way! The Gospel is in our hearts and mouths, and it is the Gospel that is the power of God for salvation (Romans 1:16).

Simon Guillebaud, a British missionary in Burundi, spoke on a Flame International online teaching about some of the things he encountered in the horrific war in Burundi while he lived there. One day he was preaching near the Congolese border, and he preached on the return of Christ (Matthew 25). Below is the conclusion of the parable which he emphasised (vs 6-12)

"At midnight the cry rang out: 'Here's the bridegroom! Come out to meet him!' Then all the virgins woke up and trimmed their lamps. The foolish ones said to the wise, 'Give us some of your oil; our lamps are going out.' 'No,' they replied, 'there may not be enough for both us and you. Instead, go to those who sell oil and buy some for yourselves.'

"But while they were on their way to buy the oil, the bridegroom arrived. The virgins who were ready went in with him to the wedding banquet. And the door was shut. "Later the others also came. 'Lord, Lord,' they said, 'open the door for us!' But he replied, 'Truly I tell you, I don't know you.'"

When Simon preached, his message was simple; **"Jesus is coming – nobody knows when – are you ready?"** Many were moved by the conviction of the Holy Spirit, and undoubtedly the fear of the Lord, to repent and believe in the Lord Jesus Christ. Simon went back there two days later, and the military had built a roadblock. When Simon asked what was going on, they told him that he could not proceed as there was a rebel attack. The people who had listened just days earlier were being killed. The sense of dreadful awe filled him as he realised that what he had said to them just a few days earlier was for many their last chance of eternal salvation. Were they ready? Had they repented and turned to Christ, or did they refuse Christ, until the point that day where they would have realised it was too late!

We too need to have a greater sense of urgency. Simon went on to say that many in the Church live in a 'peacetime' delusion, whereas actually we need to wake up to realise we are living in a war-time reality! In England, for example, we may not be living in a country torn by war, but every Christian is a member of Christ's army, and the battle is for people's souls.

I am not asking you to get your PA system and microphone out and shout about God's judgement to the local onlookers. But a question I ask you is this; does the just judgement of God on the sinner compel you to pray for the lost souls and urge you to be obedient to God's call to tell people the Good News of salvation?

I am aware that one of, if not, the main hindrance to us telling people the truth about Jesus, is fear. We might think, "What if they laugh at me, or what if they forcefully reject me? What if I am ridiculed and I'd feel embarrassed? What if I push them further away from Jesus?" The fear of man, the fear of failure, the fear of rejection, the fear of looking stupid can all prevent us from sharing the message of Christ. Joy Dawson wrote, "The fear of the Lord is the only way to be released from the fear of man." [14]

When my family and I lived in Aldershot, UK, I was moved by God with a desire to evangelise on the streets. There were many Nepalese people living there and I knew that many of them would have never heard the Gospel before, so with compassion for them I wanted to reach out. I wrote a Gospel message and got it translated into Nepalese. I went out for the first time with much fear of looking stupid. I sheepishly tried to give people these Gospel tracts and the majority were turned away. Having handed out about 4 or 5 I felt pretty humiliated and went home.

A week later I listened to an evangelistic sermon online and was gripped and empowered by the Holy Spirit that this was the right thing

---

[14] *'Intimate Friendship with God'*, by Joy Dawson, Youth With A Mission, page 33

to do. In my hand I held a tract that held the invaluable message that brings salvation. The people I had in my heart were headed for eternal darkness – they HAD to have an opportunity to receive the Truth! So I went out with a fire in my spirit, bold and convicted, and **everyone** who I approached, took the tract! I even stopped a jogger who was passing by me! It was totally opposite to the week before.

It would be good for our evangelism to be motivated with a holy fear, as well as love.

Conclusion

How to seek the fear of the Lord

Jesus says, *"Seek, and you will find."* (Matthew 7:7)

This I consider, is perhaps the most important chapter. We have read much into the fear of the Lord, but unless we seek to grow in it ourselves and apply it in our lives, it is mere head knowledge and won't produce any fruit. I hope that the Holy Spirit has been working in your heart as you have been reading this book, and at times you may have felt somewhat overwhelmed with the weight of the Spirit that you didn't know what to do. The fear of the Lord should not be a stumbling block, nor a burden too heavy to carry. The fear of the Lord is the beginning of wisdom, it brings joy, healing, protection and revelation. It is not a Pharisaic burden; it is a treasure from heaven and a gift from God to mankind.

Proverbs 2:1-5 says,

> *"My son, if you accept my words and store up my commands within you, turning your ear to wisdom and applying your heart to understanding—indeed, if you call out for insight and cry aloud for understanding, and if you look for it as for silver and search for it as for hidden treasure, then you will understand the fear of the Lord and find the knowledge of God."*

Here are some simple steps to seek the fear of the Lord.

1) If you have previously not liked the fear of the Lord and even spoken against it somehow, repent. Repent, because you have not been speaking against a theme or doctrine but undermining the character of God.

   You can say these words or similar words of your own. *Lord, I confess I have spoken badly about the fear of the Lord and therefore undermined your holy Name. I have shunned it and have not given You the honour and fear You deserve. I now choose to not speak badly against the fear of the Lord, and if somebody questions me about it, I choose to honour You by saying what Scripture declares of the importance of fearing You.*

2) If you want to have the fear of the Lord, then ask God for it. Ask as in accordance with James 1:5-6, *"If any of you lacks wisdom, you should ask God, who gives generously to all without finding fault, and it will be given to you. But when you ask, you must believe and not doubt, because the one who doubts is like a wave of the sea, blown and tossed by the wind."*

   Ask God to give you the Holy Spirit, or more of the fullness of the Holy Spirit (as the fear of the Lord is part of the sevenfold Spirit of God). "How much more will your heavenly Father give you the Holy Spirit to those who ask." (Luke 11:13).

3) Pay particular attention to it in Scripture. There are so many mentions of the fear of the Lord in Scripture. When you read them, don't pass them by quickly, but meditate on it and make sure you have taken it onboard. Perhaps start by spending time reading and meditating on Proverbs 2, and Psalm 34.

If there were Scriptures in this book which caused you to sense the fear of God, consider that through those Scriptures God was speaking to you! Spend time meditating on those Scriptures and asking for the Holy Spirit to cause that word to deeply penetrate and transform you.

4) Search for greater insight and understanding of the last days and the return of Christ. Meditate on the truth of what the Lord will do and ask God to convict you with a holy fear of His coming judgement.

5) Search what areas of your life you do not have the fear of God. You may have a holy hatred towards sex before marriage, but do you have a holy hatred towards grumbling against other people, particularly other believers? Search your heart and be aware of where the Holy Spirit reveals there is a lack of godly fear. When you know this, then ask God to give you the fear of God over this area of your life. Then make intentional effort to resist the devil from that temptation. When you feel tempted to sin in that area, resist the devil using the Word of God. "I will not do that sin, because my Father in Heaven hates it and He tells me not to commit it." A scripture that I find helpful to speak out against the devil in times of temptation is, "It is written, *"The acts of the flesh are obvious: sexual immorality, impurity and debauchery; idolatry and witchcraft; hatred, discord, jealousy, fits of rage, selfish ambition, dissensions, factions and envy; drunkenness, orgies, and the like. I warn you, as I did before, that those who live like this will not inherit the kingdom of God."* (Galatians 5:19-21).

If you are struggling in an area of sin, find accountability. Tell someone you trust about it. "Confess your sins to one another and be healed." (James 5:16).

6) In a time of prayer, ask God "Show me what you hate." This can be a very powerful way to come into more alignment with His heart and holiness (see Chapter 20).

7) Pursue God in times of worship. I express in Chapter 16 the importance of worship. Spend time with your face on the floor, crying out "Holy, holy, holy is the Lord God Almighty." This is humbling and can open our hearts to holy revelation of Him.

I finish off with this prayer for you in my own words, encouraged by Psalm 67.

May God Our Father, through the Lord Jesus Christ be gracious to you and bless you with a growing awareness of His glory and His holiness. May God pour out for you the Spirit of the fear of the Lord, that you will truly honour Christ in your lives. May Christ reign in your whole being so that the world around you will learn the ways of God, and those you meet with will come to know His salvation. May Christ in you convince others to grow in righteousness and praise, that people from the whole world will learn to fear God and worship Him alone. Amen.

Appendix 1: The Parables

Parable of The Net (Matthew 13:47-50)

"Once again, the kingdom of heaven is like a net that was let down into the lake and caught all kinds of fish. When it was full, the fishermen pulled it up on the shore. Then they sat down and collected the good fish in baskets, but threw the bad away. This is how it will be at the end of the age. The angels will come and separate the wicked from the righteous and throw them into the blazing furnace, where there will be weeping and gnashing of teeth."

Parable of The Weeds Among the Wheat (Matthew 13:24-30)

"Jesus told them another parable: The kingdom of heaven is like a man who sowed good seed in his field. But while everyone was sleeping, his enemy came and sowed weeds among the wheat, and went away. When the wheat sprouted and formed heads, then the weeds also appeared. The owner's servants came to him and said, 'Sir, didn't you sow good seed in your field? Where then did the weeds come from?'

"'An enemy did this,' he replied.

"The servants asked him, 'Do you want us to go and pull them up?'

"'No,' he answered, 'because while you are pulling the weeds, you may uproot the wheat with them. Let both grow together until the harvest. At that time I will tell the harvesters: First collect the weeds and tie them in bundles to be burned; then gather the wheat and bring it into my barn.'"

Parable of The Unforgiving Servant (Matthew 18:23-35)

"Therefore, the kingdom of heaven is like a king who wanted to settle accounts with his servants. As he began the settlement, a man who owed him ten thousand bags of gold was brought to him. Since he was not able to pay, the master ordered that he and his wife and his children and all that he had be sold to repay the debt.

"At this the servant fell on his knees before him. 'Be patient with me,' he begged, 'and I will pay back everything.' The servant's master took pity on him, cancelled the debt and let him go.

"But when that servant went out, he found one of his fellow servants who owed him a hundred silver coins. He grabbed him and began to choke him. 'Pay back what you owe me!' he demanded.

"His fellow servant fell to his knees and begged him, 'Be patient with me, and I will pay it back.'

"But he refused. Instead, he went off and had the man thrown into prison until he could pay the debt. When the other servants saw what had happened, they were outraged and went and told their master everything that had happened.

"Then the master called the servant in. 'You wicked servant,' he said, 'I canceled all that debt of yours because you begged me to. Shouldn't you have had mercy on your fellow servant just as I had on you?' In anger his master handed him over to the jailers to be tortured, until he should pay back all he owed.

"This is how my heavenly Father will treat each of you unless you forgive your brother or sister from your heart."

Parable of the Marriage Feast (Matthew 22:1-14)

"Jesus spoke to them again in parables, saying: 'The kingdom of heaven is like a king who prepared a wedding banquet for his son. He sent his servants to

those who had been invited to the banquet to tell them to come, but they refused to come.'

"Then he sent some more servants and said, 'Tell those who have been invited that I have prepared my dinner: My oxen and fattened cattle have been butchered, and everything is ready. Come to the wedding banquet.'

"But they paid no attention and went off—one to his field, another to his business. The rest seized his servants, mistreated them and killed them. The king was enraged. He sent his army and destroyed those murderers and burned their city.

"Then he said to his servants, 'The wedding banquet is ready, but those I invited did not deserve to come. So go to the street corners and invite to the banquet anyone you find.' So the servants went out into the streets and gathered all the people they could find, the bad as well as the good, and the wedding hall was filled with guests.

"But when the king came in to see the guests, he noticed a man there who was not wearing wedding clothes. He asked, 'How did you get in here without wedding clothes, friend?' The man was speechless.

"Then the king told the attendants, 'Tie him hand and foot, and throw him outside, into the darkness, where there will be weeping and gnashing of teeth.'

"For many are invited, but few are chosen."

Parable of Faithful vs. Wicked Servant (Matthew 24:45-51)

"Who then is the faithful and wise servant, whom the master has put in charge of the servants in his household to give them their food at the proper time? It will be good for that servant whose master finds him doing so when he returns. Truly I tell you, he will put him in charge of all his possessions. But suppose *that servant is wicked and says to himself, 'My master is staying away a long time,' and he then begins to beat his fellow servants and to eat and drink with drunkards. The master of that servant will come on a day when he does not expect him and at an hour he is not aware of. He will cut him to pieces and assign him a place with the hypocrites, where there will be weeping and gnashing of teeth."*

Parable of The Ten Virgins (Matthew 25:1-13)

"At that time the kingdom of heaven will be like ten virgins who took their lamps and went out to meet the bridegroom. Five of them were foolish and five were wise. The foolish ones took their lamps but did not take any oil with them. The wise ones, however, took oil in jars along with their lamps. The bridegroom was a long time in coming, and they all became drowsy and fell asleep.

"At midnight the cry rang out: 'Here's the bridegroom! Come out to meet him!'

"Then all the virgins woke up and trimmed their lamps. The foolish ones said to the wise, 'Give us some of your oil; our lamps are going out.'

"'No,' they replied, 'there may not be enough for both us and you. Instead, go to those who sell oil and buy some for yourselves.'

"But while they were on their way to buy the oil, the bridegroom arrived. The virgins who were ready went in with him to the wedding banquet. And the door was shut.

"Later the others also came. 'Lord, Lord,' they said, 'open the door for us!'

"But he replied, 'Truly I tell you, I don't know you.'

"Therefore keep watch, because you do not know the day or the hour."

Parable of Ten Talents (Matthew 25:14-30)

"Again, it will be like a man going on a journey, who called his servants and entrusted his wealth to them. To one he gave five bags of gold, to another two bags, and to another one bag, each according to his ability. Then he went on his journey. The man who had received five bags of gold went at once and put his money to work and gained five bags more. So also, the one with two bags of gold gained two more. But the man who had received one bag went off, dug a hole in the ground and hid his master's money.

"After a long time the master of those servants returned and settled accounts with them. The man who had received five bags of gold brought the other five. 'Master,' he said, 'you entrusted me with five bags of gold. See, I have gained five more.'

"His master replied, 'Well done, good and faithful servant! You have been faithful with a few things; I will put you in charge of many things. Come and share your master's happiness!'

"The man with two bags of gold also came. 'Master,' he said, 'you entrusted me with two bags of gold; see, I have gained two more.'

"His master replied, 'Well done, good and faithful servant! You have been faithful with a few things; I will put you in charge of many things. Come and share your master's happiness!'

"Then the man who had received one bag of gold came. 'Master,' he said, 'I knew that you are a hard man, harvesting where you have not sown and gathering where you have not scattered seed. So I was afraid and went out and hid your gold in the ground. See, here is what belongs to you.'

"His master replied, 'You wicked, lazy servant! So you knew that I harvest where I have not sown and gather where I have not scattered seed? Well then, you should have put my money on deposit with the bankers, so that when I returned I would have received it back with interest.

"'So take the bag of gold from him and give it to the one who has ten bags. For whoever has will be given more, and they will have an abundance. Whoever does not have, even what they have will be taken from them. And throw that worthless servant outside, into the darkness, where there will be weeping and gnashing of teeth.'"

www.ingramcontent.com/pod-product-compliance
Lightning Source LLC
Chambersburg PA
CBHW061220070526
44584CB00029B/3913